OPPOSING
VIEWPOINTS®
SERIES

Scientific Research

Other Books of Related Interest

Opposing Viewpoints Series

The Aging Population

Human Genetics

Nanotechnology

Performance-Enhancing Drugs

At Issue Series

Animal Experimentation

Extending the Human Lifespan

Genetically Modified Food

Vaccines

Current Controversies Series

Abortion

Animal Rights

Medical Ethics

Prescription Drugs

"Congress shall make
no law . . . abridging
the freedom of speech,
or of the press."

First Amendment to the US Constitution

The basic foundation of our democracy is the First Amendment guarantee of freedom of expression. The Opposing Viewpoints series is dedicated to the concept of this basic freedom and the idea that it is more important to practice it than to enshrine it.

OPPOSING VIEWPOINTS® SERIES

Scientific Research

Sylvia Engdahl, Book Editor

GREENHAVEN PRESS
A part of Gale, Cengage Learning

GALE
CENGAGE Learning·

Farmington Hills, Mich • San Francisco • New York • Waterville, Maine
Meriden, Conn • Mason, Ohio • Chicago

GALE
CENGAGE Learning

Patricia Coryell, *Vice President & Publisher, New Products & GVRL*
Douglas Dentino, *Manager, New Products*
Judy Galens, *Acquisitions Editor*

For more information, contact:
Greenhaven Press
27500 Drake Rd.
Farmington Hills, MI 48331-3535
Or you can visit our Internet site at gale.cengage.com

For product information and technology assistance, contact us at

Gale Customer Support, 1-800-877-4253
For permission to use material from this text or product, submit all requests online at www.cengage.com/permissions

Further permissions questions can be emailed to permissionrequest@cengage.com

Articles in Greenhaven Press anthologies are often edited for length to meet page requirements. In addition, original titles of these works are changed to clearly present the main thesis and to explicitly indicate the author's opinion. Every effort is made to ensure that Greenhaven Press accurately reflects the original intent of the authors. Every effort has been made to trace the owners of copyrighted material.

Cover Image copyright © Alexander Raths/Shutterstock.com.

LIBRARY OF CONGRESS CATALOGING-IN-PUBLICATION DATA

Scientific research (Greenhaven Press)
Scientific research / Sylvia Engdahl, book editor.
        pages cm. -- (Opposing viewpoints)
    Includes bibliographical references and index.
    ISBN 978-0-7377-7288-3 (hardback) -- ISBN 978-0-7377-7289-0 (paperback)
    1. Research. 2. Research--Social aspects. 3. Research--Moral and ethical aspects.
 I. Engdahl, Sylvia, editor. II. Title.
    Q180.A1S357 2015
    507.2--dc23
                                                                        2014032837

Printed in the United States of America
1 2 3 4 5 6 7 19 18 17 16 15

Contents

Chapter 3: Should Animals Be Used in Scientific Research?

Chapter 4: Are Fraud and Misconduct by Scientists Common?

Why Consider Opposing Viewpoints?

> *"The only way in which a human being can make some approach to knowing the whole of a subject is by hearing what can be said about it by persons of every variety of opinion and studying all modes in which it can be looked at by every character of mind. No wise man ever acquired his wisdom in any mode but this."*
>
> *John Stuart Mill*

In our media-intensive culture it is not difficult to find differing opinions. Thousands of newspapers and magazines and dozens of radio and television talk shows resound with differing points of view. The difficulty lies in deciding which opinion to agree with and which "experts" seem the most credible. The more inundated we become with differing opinions and claims, the more essential it is to hone critical reading and thinking skills to evaluate these ideas. Opposing Viewpoints books address this problem directly by presenting stimulating debates that can be used to enhance and teach these skills. The varied opinions contained in each book examine many different aspects of a single issue. While examining these conveniently edited opposing views, readers can develop critical thinking skills such as the ability to compare and contrast authors' credibility, facts, argumentation styles, use of persuasive techniques, and other stylistic tools. In short, the Opposing Viewpoints Series is an ideal way to attain the higher-level thinking and reading skills so essential in a culture of diverse and contradictory opinions.

In addition to providing a tool for critical thinking, Opposing Viewpoints books challenge readers to question their own strongly held opinions and assumptions. Most people form their opinions on the basis of upbringing, peer pressure, and personal, cultural, or professional bias. By reading carefully balanced opposing views, readers must directly confront new ideas as well as the opinions of those with whom they disagree. This is not to argue simplistically that everyone who reads opposing views will—or should—change his or her opinion. Instead, the series enhances readers' understanding of their own views by encouraging confrontation with opposing ideas. Careful examination of others' views can lead to the readers' understanding of the logical inconsistencies in their own opinions, perspective on why they hold an opinion, and the consideration of the possibility that their opinion requires further evaluation.

Evaluating Other Opinions

To ensure that this type of examination occurs, Opposing Viewpoints books present all types of opinions. Prominent spokespeople on different sides of each issue as well as well-known professionals from many disciplines challenge the reader. An additional goal of the series is to provide a forum for other, less known, or even unpopular viewpoints. The opinion of an ordinary person who has had to make the decision to cut off life support from a terminally ill relative, for example, may be just as valuable and provide just as much insight as a medical ethicist's professional opinion. The editors have two additional purposes in including these less known views. One, the editors encourage readers to respect others' opinions—even when not enhanced by professional credibility. It is only by reading or listening to and objectively evaluating others' ideas that one can determine whether they are worthy of consideration. Two, the inclusion of such viewpoints encourages the important critical thinking skill of objectively evaluating an author's credentials and bias. This evaluation will illuminate an author's reasons for taking a particular stance on an issue and will aid in readers' evaluation of the author's ideas.

It is our hope that these books will give readers a deeper understanding of the issues debated and an appreciation of the complexity of even seemingly simple issues when good and honest people disagree. This awareness is particularly important in a democratic society such as ours in which people enter into public debate to determine the common good. Those with whom one disagrees should not be regarded as enemies but rather as people whose views deserve careful examination and may shed light on one's own.

Thomas Jefferson once said that "difference of opinion leads to inquiry, and inquiry to truth." Jefferson, a broadly educated man, argued that "if a nation expects to be ignorant and free . . . it expects what never was and never will be." As individuals and as a nation, it is imperative that we consider the opinions of others and examine them with skill and discernment. The Opposing Viewpoints series is intended to help readers achieve this goal.

David L. Bender and Bruno Leone,
Founders

Introduction

> *"Scientific innovation ... has offered us benefits that have improved our health and our lives—improvements we take too easily for granted. But it gives us something more. At root, science forces us to reckon with the truth as best as we can ascertain it. ... Science cannot supplant our ethics or our values, our principles or our faith. But science can inform those things and help put those values—these moral sentiments, that faith—can put those things to work—to feed a child, or to heal the sick, to be good stewards of this Earth."*
>
> —Barack Obama,
> *Remarks at the National Academy
> of Sciences, April 27, 2009*

Most people are aware of the great benefits science provides to society, and many are deeply interested in reading about scientific discoveries. Scientists have generally been admired and have been pictured as devoting a significant amount of time during their working lives to making such discoveries, with little concern for more mundane activities.

Professor of education Vasilia Christidou, in the April 2011 issue of the *International Journal of Environmental and Science Education*, reports that a mid-twentieth century study of high school students' attitudes toward science showed that they have "a stereotypic and complex perception of scientists as elderly or middle aged men, who wear glasses and/or beards and work in laboratories surrounded by equipment—test tubes, Bunsen burners, flasks and bottles—taking notes and reading books. One day the scientist may straighten up and shout: 'I've found it!'"

By now this view is less prevalent; the public realizes that the vast majority of scientists are ordinary men and women engaged in ongoing work at which they happen to excel. At the same time, society's feeling toward scientists has become more ambivalent. In 2012, writing in the journal *Genome Biology*, biochemist Gregory Petsko noted, "Public perception of science has shifted in recent decades from one of the scientist as savior to one in which we are seen by many to be self-absorbed glory-hounds, more interested in the pursuit of discovery and the rewards it brings than we are in the consequences our work may have for the well-being of society."

It cannot be denied that this may be true of a minority of researchers, for as the purview of science has grown and the population has increased, inevitably some people with self-serving motives have sought careers in science, just as is the case with all professions. Furthermore, the path to career advancement in science is not always compatible with devotion to a search for ways to benefit humankind.

Moreover, work on today's advanced scientific projects requires complex laboratory equipment, supplies, and salaried assistants—all of which cost a great deal of money. Gone are the days when a scientist working alone in a personal lab could make significant discoveries. Scientists need funding, and most funds come either from the government, which is influenced by political considerations, or from private industry, which supports projects mainly on the basis of their commercial value. On top of these biases, there is often rivalry within academia and a tendency to support only those scientists who agree with the theories of their superiors.

Neuroscientist Giovanni Frazzetto, in an article titled "The Changing Identity of the Scientist," in the January 2004 edition of *EMBO Reports*, writes, "Scientists have created complex alliances between academia and industry, with the boundaries between science, politics and economics becoming increasingly indistinct. This development has also brought about disenchantment with what is by now an almost utopian vision of scientific practice based on the virtuous pursuit of objectivity, universalism, disinterestedness and impersonality."

The greatest source of ambivalence toward scientists, however, lies not so much in the public perception of them as in society's ambivalence toward science itself. Science and technology have provided all the advances on which modern civilization depends. However, it also has brought much that can, or could in the future, be used for ill-intended purposes as well as for good. There has always been suspicion, expressed in popular fiction such as *Frankenstein*, that not all science is benign. Beginning with the creation of the atomic bomb, this suspicion has grown. Nuclear power, genetic engineering, biotechnology, nanotechnology, neuroscience, artificial intelligence, geoengineering, and even medical research are fields with potential for abuse. Some people fear the negative consequences of such discoveries so much that they lose sight of the positive aspects and blame "science" for endangering the world while relying on its benefits in their daily lives.

Nevertheless, few would say that scientific research is not essential to society. The significant controversies surrounding scientific research concern not its value, but how it should be conducted. The authors in *Opposing Viewpoints: Scientific Research* offer differing opinions about some of the controversies in chapters titled "Should the Government Fund Scientific Research?," "Is There Too Much Regulation of Scientific Research?," "Should Animals Be Used in Scientific Research?," and "Are Fraud and Misconduct by Scientists Common?" These issues have bearing on how scientists work and whether problems not related to the work itself will get in the way of scientists' success in gaining new knowledge.

OPPOSING
VIEWPOINTS®
SERIES

Should the Government Fund Scientific Research?

Chapter Preface

On May 29, 2014, the Committee on Science, Space, and Technology of the US House of Representatives approved the Frontiers in Innovation, Research, Science, and Technology (FIRST) Act. In addition to reauthorizing funding for the National Science Foundation (NSF), this bill prioritizes physical and biological sciences ahead of social sciences and, in the words of Cornell University president David J. Skorton, adds a "potentially devastating layer of review to ensure any research is 'worthy of federal funding' and 'in the national interest.'"

The fundamental issue raised by this bill is wider than the relative importance of various fields of research. "When politicians become involved, we risk letting politics trump scientific merit," wrote David Takeuchi, associate dean for research at the Boston College School of Social Work, in the May 29, 2014, issue of the *Boston Globe*. "FIRST stipulates that each NSF research grant be subject to congressional certification that the project 'is in the national interest.' But all this means is that politicians would have the opportunity to cherry-pick the studies they believe hold some kind of interest—national, personal, political, or otherwise."

Yet the bill's supporters point out that without oversight, a great deal of taxpayers' money has been spent—and in the eyes of some, wasted—on trivial studies that contribute little, if anything, to the public good. Representative Lamar Smith, chairman of the House Committee on Science, Space and Technology, told *Scientific American*, "There is understandable resistance to congressional policy making from those who prefer NSF's funding to come without having to answer questions from Congress or the taxpayers. Under this approach NSF has lavished funds on what can be described charitably as questionable projects." He added, "It's not the government's money, it's the people's money. And it's the role of Congress to set priorities for research that are in the national interest."

To be sure, it requires some knowledge of science to pass judgment on projects that to the uninformed may sound insignificant. In criticizing scientific research of dubious public value, the former governor of Alaska and vice presidential candidate Sarah Palin famously said, "Things like fruit fly research in Paris, France. I kid you not." In reality, the study of fruit flies over a long period has been crucial to the understanding of how genes work; it is a prime example of basic research with major impact on scientific progress. However, many other projects are funded with little justification apart from an individual scientist's curiosity, or worse, his or her desire to publish for the sake of career advancement. Some are also motivated by political considerations.

Where should the line be drawn? Some projects that seem useless even to a researcher's fellow scientists turn out to have far-reaching consequences. For example, physicist Charles Townes received the Nobel Prize for research on microwaves that eventually led to the invention of the laser—work that many of his colleagues had originally called a waste of time and money. A $250,000 study of the mating habits of the screwworm, initially ridiculed by the press, resulted in discovery of a way to eradicate the parasite, thereby saving the cattle industry more than $20 billion.

Not all work done with federal grant money is potentially significant, however. Senator Tom Coburn, in his widely criticized report "The National Science Foundation: Under the Microscope," describes studies he thinks should not have received grants—including, among others, those on how quickly American parents respond to trendy baby names and why the same basketball teams always dominate the National Collegiate Athletic Association (NCAA) tournament. "It is not the intent of this report to suggest that there is no utility associated with these research efforts," he wrote. "The overarching question to ask, however, is simple. Are these projects the best possible use of our tax dollars?"

That question is more fundamental than the issue of whether Congress should decide how the NSF spends its funds. Many people do not believe the government should fund science at all—not because they doubt the value of science but because they consider private funding preferable. The authors in this chapter offer differing views on how science should be funded.

| "Cutting science funding is a way of killing our future."

Government-Funded Scientific Research Is an Investment in the Future

Annalee Newitz

In the following viewpoint, Annalee Newitz discusses recent cuts in government funding of scientific research and the harm she believes will result from such cuts. She refutes several myths commonly used as arguments against government science funding: that it is a partisan issue; that it results in useless or questionable research; and that private funders will fill in the gaps if government funding is cut. She also points out that government funding provides a check on the biases of privately funded research. Newitz is a widely published journalist and the editor in chief of the science blog io9.

As you read, consider the following questions:

1. According to Newitz, what is the main reason public funding of science is threatened?

2. Why, according to Newitz, is it wrong to consider science funding a partisan issue?

3. Why, in Newitz's opinion, will private investors not make up for cuts in public science funding?

Did you use a browser to zoom around on the Internet today? Have you ever been vaccinated? If you answered yes to either of those questions, your life has already been made better through publicly funded science in America. Public science is basic scientific research funded by governments, and just in America alone it's led to breakthroughs in everything from medicine to clean energy. But now public science is under threat. Here's why—and why we can't afford to lose it.

The US government has pledged to deal with the nation's debt crisis by cutting social spending. On the chopping block are many many social programs, including some of the country's most important government-funded science institutions like the National Science Foundation (NSF), National Institutes of Health (NIH), and the National Oceanic and Atmospheric Administration (NOAA).

NASA's [National Aeronautics and Space Administration] budget has already been slashed, eliminating thousands of jobs and threatening to kill the launch of the James Webb telescope that would replace the aging Hubble. NSF funding was cut this year [2011] by $53 million. President [Barack] Obama's requests for a larger NSF budget have been turned down for 2011 and 2012—in fact, NSF funds were cut in 2011 down to $6.81 billion for the year, despite Obama's request for a billion-dollar funding boost.

As *Nature* reported earlier this month, science agencies are already set to lose money in 2012. Some areas of research will hurt more than others—more money will be allocated to projects on "cybersecurity," for example, while funding for climate research at NOAA will be cut. In addition, science agencies face even steeper cuts in 2013 and 2014, when the next round of budget cuts is slated to take effect. . . .

Cutting science funding is a way of killing our future. And yet there are a number of political arguments in favor of cutting science funding—some of which are myths based on ideology or misunderstandings rather than facts. We deal with a few of these below.

MYTH: Public science is a partisan issue, and Republicans have always opposed science funding in America.

FACT: Historically, Republicans have been on the forefront of creating public funds for basic science research. One of the agencies that's most endangered by budget cuts, the Environmental Protection Agency (EPA), was established by Republican president Richard Nixon. Though this agency has done some of the most important work to uncover the dangers of environmental hazards like the growing ozone hole, Democratic president Barack Obama argued just over a week ago that key elements of the agency's work need to go.

The National Science Foundation has been a darling of Republicans since its founding in the 1950s. Under Ronald Reagan in the 1980s, funding for NSF doubled, and the administration praised the role of basic science research. Indeed, the last time we saw cuts to science funding comparable to those over the past few years, it was during the Democratic [Bill] Clinton administration.

Today, some politicians are arguing that science funding should bear the brunt of the coming budget cuts. Republican senator Tom Coburn has sponsored an extensive study of how NSF's funding is "wasteful." But many politicians, from both parties, still support science funding, and historically Republicans have worked hand in hand with Democrats to expand budgets for science research of all kinds, from environmental science to medicine.

MYTH: Grants from publicly funded agencies like NSF and NIH wind up funding useless and questionable forms of research.

FACT: Over the past couple of years, politicians have been calling out government-funded science, claiming that taxpayer money is going into dubious scientific pursuits. Let's address a few of them.

Recently, there was a media scandal over how the NIH had supposedly funded a study on "gay men's penis sizes." A number of news organizations reported the news as fact, when not only was it a misrepresentation of the study—which was focused on gay male sexual health—but also was not funded by the NIH. The researcher who conducted the study was funded by the NIH for other projects leading to his advanced degree, but his study of gay men's health was done on his own time. This kind of kerfuffle is a result of a profound misunderstanding of how funding works. Many graduate students in the sciences get funding to complete their degrees from the NIH and NSF, among other agencies. But they also conduct research on their own, related to their chosen field of study but not required to receive a degree. Receiving money from a government funding agency does not mean that all research you do is funded by the government.

Meanwhile, in his NSF report, Senator Coburn argues that we should cut NSF because NSF-funded researchers at McMurdo Station in Antarctica are known to spend their spare time Jell-O wrestling. He's referring to a single incident, where an official at McMurdo was fired for organizing a Jell-O wrestling match among the small crew of researchers who spend the year in Antarctica studying everything from astrophysics and earth sciences, to zoology and paleontology. One ill-advised off-duty incident doesn't prove that the station's research is wasteful.

Here's the truth: The NIH has funded research that led to 130 Nobel Prizes, and recently funded research that led to the

Government Support of Scientific Research Is Vital

Our world is an ever-changing environment, and it is naïve to think that any country can conduct business as it has been and expect that to be adequate for the future. While the US can pride itself on a legacy of remarkable advancements, it is time once again to reexamine what policies and resources are available for the future. We must examine the question: "What role is the US playing now, and what role will it play in the future of international science?" The US is facing increasing global competition in research and research-related areas. . . .

In addition, given the results of our analysis, we must consider, "How will the US continue to foster its scientific strengths?" These results illustrate that the US financial commitment to research has plateaued in recent years, although the federal government has shifted more of its funding toward basic and applied research, while industry continues to concentrate on development. As science is founded on rigor and quality, it will be a mistake to be distracted by sheer quantity. . . .

Research (both basic and applied) translates into technological innovations that, in turn, transform into benefits for society and improvements in people's lives. Given that a substantial increase in funding is unlikely, the US government will have to find new innovative ways to increase the effectiveness of current funding. . . . As the 21st century moves ahead, it is vital that the federal government continues and strengthens its support of research and formulates a thoughtful and competitive science policy for this new century.

Gregory J. Hather et al., "The United States of America and Scientific Research," PLoS ONE, August 16, 2010.

first cancer vaccine.... And the NSF has sponsored research that led to 180 Nobel Prizes. Over the past few years, NSF has contributed to research that has made major strides in health, energy efficiency, and exploration. The NSF funded one of the very first web browsers in the 1990s, and is currently funding the development of next-generation robotics. NSF and its sister science agencies are investing in technologies that could one day transform the world.

MYTH: If we cut government spending on the sciences, private funders will step up to fill in the gaps, and they'll do it without all that wasteful spending.

FACT: Private investors fuel innovation all the time, but the very nature of business investments precludes most investors' ability to pay for basic research. Investors usually need a return on their investments in the short term, and most basic research projects take decades to result in something that can be sold in the marketplace—indeed, some kinds of research, like space travel, may require generations before they become profitable. And research into atmospheric changes may save the human species, but never make any money at all.

The other problem with private funding is that it can bias basic research. In the 1990s, tobacco industry leader Philip Morris funded scientific studies "proving" that smoking isn't harmful, and tried to legislate away studies that showed the harms. And pharmaceutical company GlaxoSmithKline was sued in New York for fraud because the company didn't release data showing their best-selling drug, Paxil, increased the risk of suicide in young people (the company settled). The point is that corporations naturally have their own interests to protect—interests that can't underwrite open, basic science research.

Government-funded science isn't exactly bias free, but it can, and has, provided a check on the biases of privately funded science. Basic scientific research is a public good, like education and roads. It is a long-term investment in our country's future, and the future of our planet.

> "It seems unreasonable to assume that the private market will satisfy the research demands that an ever-evolving society requires."

Government Funding of Scientific Research Is Essential to the Public Good

Oliver Tonkin

In the following viewpoint, Oliver Tonkin argues that federally funded scientific research conducted by universities is necessary because private industry can rarely be persuaded to invest in long-term, low-return research. Basic research, he says, seeks the public good and a better understanding of the world, while applied research focuses on practical applications—that is, on research that can be monetized. Although basic research contributes significantly to the growth of the economy, only a small percentage of the research conducted by industries is basic research; therefore, in Tonkin's opinion, much less of it would be carried out if government funding were eliminated. Tonkin is a political science and global studies major at the University of Nebraska.

As you read, consider the following questions:

1. What percentage of basic scientific research was funded by the federal government in 2006, according to Tonkin?

2. What evidence does Tonkin offer to support the statement that privately funded basic research is decreasing?

3. Why might private funding of scientific research be detrimental to public health policy, according to Tonkin?

University research significantly contributes to the ever-increasing body of knowledge leading to social and economic improvements. Federally funded research to universities is necessary to ensure the long-term viability of American leadership in innovation and social progress. Federal funds are responsible for the development of the Internet, GPS [global positioning system], touch screens, MRI [magnetic resonance imaging] and lifesaving vaccines, as well as positive growth for jobs and productivity. Privately funded research, on the other hand, would shift the focus from the public good to profitability.

It seems unreasonable to assume that the private market will satisfy the research demands that an ever-evolving society requires, particularly when it considers public goods that offer little chance for profitability. Rarely will corporations be persuaded to invest in long-term, low-return research. Privately funded research is less objective and focuses on research that can be monetized. When the private market allows for a deficit of public goods to occur, it is the government's responsibility to meet that demand. Replacing federal funding to universities with corporate funding would degrade the public good.

One central argument focuses on the benefits of basic research as opposed to applied research. Basic research is the pursuit of a better understanding of the world and the public good, whereas applied research seeks practical implementation of research, often into the marketplace. The international research community as a whole agrees that basic research is interdependent on innovation and the manifestation of research into products in the marketplace.

According to the National Science Foundation, of the $340 billion spent on research in 2006, $62 billion of it was basic research (18 percent). The federal government funds 59 percent of basic research, mostly conducted by academic institutions. Only 3.8 percent of industry-funded research is basic research. If this ratio stays true in replacing funding for universities, then there would be nearly $50 billion less invested in basic research.

Privately Funded Basic Research Is Decreasing

The presence of businesses in basic research is dwindling, according to the National Science Foundation, the independent federal agency that funds much of university research. Privately financed physical and biomedical sciences publications have decreased since 2000.

Industry-funded research articles in peer-reviewed journals have also decreased, indicating a prioritization of monetizing the fruits of research over promoting the public good. Yes, that's precisely what businesses ought to do in a market economy. That is exactly why federal funding for universities is necessary. Academia should not act as the vehicle for businesses' profit-mongering. If corporation funding replaces federal funding in the university setting, more applied research on preferred projects with a likely biased outcome that can be monetized will become the focus.

The journal *PLOS Medicine* conducted a study that found bias exists in the way corporations pursue research studies. They target individuals and universities that appear friendly to the corporation in the hope the study will find a favorable result. In other words, companies tend to fund projects that would benefit their enterprise. More ominously, *PLOS Medi-*

cine found that studies are more likely to conclude in favor of the sponsoring company, which could have detrimental implications for public health policy.

One such example, as reported by the *American Journal of Public Health* in 2003, found that authors who had a favorable finding for a company were 80 percent more likely to have a financial relationship with the company, as opposed to 21 percent for neutral authors and 11 percent for unfavorable authors. The journal concluded by stating "noncommercial funding may be more essential to maintaining objectivity than disclosing personal financial interests."

Some noncommercial examples include benefactors and organizations such as the Bill and Melinda Gates Foundation, which fund research in purely philanthropic ways. Their motivation is neither power, nor profit, but a genuine interest in promoting the public good. Their participation in the research realm is welcome.

Privately Funded Research Cannot Replace Federal Funding

Opponents argue that privately funded research fuels innovation and economic growth.

Companies do have an incentive to innovate in order to profit; however, once they achieve that, they will protect their products at the expense of said innovation. Industry has a place beyond their internal research and development departments. They contribute to economic progress, but it must not replace federal funding to universities and other researchers.

The Science Coalition, a nonprofit, nonpartisan organization of many universities, of which the University of Nebraska-Lincoln is a member, found that basic research significantly contributes to the growth of the economy. Hundreds of companies have originated from university research, and they succeed more often than normal start-ups based on average length in business. For example, at Stanford, Larry Page and Sergey

Percentage of People Who View Government Investment in Research as "Essential"

	Government investment is essential	Private investment is enough
Total public	60%	29%
18–29	66%	24%
30–49	63%	27%
50–64	60%	32%
65+	50%	34%
College grad +	67%	27%
Some college	65%	29%
High school or less	55%	30%
Conservative Republican	44%	48%
Moderate/Liberal Republican	56%	32%
Independent	59%	30%
Conservative/Moderate Democrat	70%	22%
Liberal Democrat	75%	19%

TAKEN FROM: "Public Praises Science; Scientists Fault Public, Media," Pew Research Center, July 9, 2009.

Brin worked on basic research on a National Science Foundation grant that sparked the idea of Google.

While private corporations seek to create proprietary standards with which to monetize their investments, government-funded researchers have virtues in intellectual curiosity and a desire to improve the world. Universities offer a platform for professional academics and researchers that isn't easily replicated elsewhere. Those who wish to devote their careers toward benevolent means can do so more easily in a university setting. However, government funding is often a prerequisite for such research to occur.

While the federal government has reduced its contribution to research funding because of the sequestration [across-the-board reduction of government spending], having corporations fill the gap is not the solution. Corporations are less an agent of social progress than they are of economic superiority. Publicly traded corporations are required by law to attempt to maximize profits on a quarterly basis. They focus on what benefits them rather than what benefits society. The public good relies on objective basic research, something only non-commercial federally funding can reliably provide.

> *"Public choice influences on science are pervasive and enforced through the massive and entrenched bureaucracies of higher education."*

Government Funding Lowers the Quality of Scientific Research

Patrick J. Michaels

In the following viewpoint, Patrick J. Michaels argues that political influences on government-funded scientific research are much greater than people generally realize. Universities spend grant money not only on support of the researchers involved but also on other academic projects, he says, and they are dependent on making sure the government funds more research in fields considered politically important. He speculates that an administrator or a scientist whose work suggests that a popular scientific issue is less important to society than it is said to be would not keep his position for long and that published research is therefore biased. Michaels is the director of the Center for the Study of Science at the Cato Institute and a past president of the American Association of State Climatologists. He is the author or editor of six books.

As you read, consider the following questions:

1. What common belief about scientific research does Michaels consider a myth?

2. According to Michaels, what percentage of scientific grant money to universities exceeds the actual cost of employing the scientists involved in the project?

3. Why do both scientists and public officials exaggerate the importance of research on global warming, according to Michaels?

Terence Kealey's insightful essay [in the August 5, 2013, issue of *Cato Unbound*] is likely to provoke a vigorous debate among libertarians on the utility of publicly funded science. He concludes that "the public funding of research has no beneficial effects on the economy." I will argue that the situation, at least in a prominent environmental science, is worse, inasmuch as the more public money is disbursed, the poorer the quality of the science, and that there is a direct cause-and-effect relationship.

This is counter to the reigning myth that science, as a search for pure truth, is ultimately immune from incentivized distortion. In fact, at one time James M. Buchanan clearly stated that he thought science was one of the few areas that was not subject to public choice influences. In his 1985 essay "The Myth of Benevolence," Buchanan wrote:

> Science is a social activity pursued by persons who acknowledge the existence of a nonindividualistic, mutually agreed-on value, namely *truth*. . . . Science cannot, therefore, be modelled in the contractarian, or exchange, paradigm.

In reality, public choice influences on science are pervasive and enforced through the massive and entrenched bureaucracies of higher education. The point of origin is probably President Franklin Roosevelt's November 17, 1944, letter to Vannevar Bush, who, as director of the wartime Office of Scientific Research and Development, managed and oversaw the Manhattan Project.

Roosevelt expressed a clear desire to expand the reach of the government far beyond theoretical and applied physics, specifically asking Bush, "What can the Government do now and in the future to aid research activities by public and private organizations." In response, in July, 1945, Bush published *Science: The Endless Frontier*, in which he explicitly acknowledged Roosevelt's more inclusive vision, saying, "It is clear from President Roosevelt's letter that in speaking of science that he had in mind the natural sciences, including biology and medicine. . . ."

A Bonanza for Universities

Bush's 1945 report explicitly laid the groundwork for the National Science Foundation, the modern incarnation of the National Institutes of Health, and the proliferation of federal science support through various federal agencies. But, instead of employing scientists directly as the Manhattan Project did, Bush proposed disbursing research support to individuals via their academic employers.

Universities saw this as a bonanza, adding substantial additional costs. A typical public university imposes a 50% surcharge on salaries and fringe benefits (at private universities the rate can approach 70%).

These fungible funds often support faculty in the many university departments that do not recover all of their costs; thus does the Physics Department often support, say, Germanic Languages. As a result, the universities suddenly became wards of the federal government and in the thrall of extensive programmatic funding. The roots of statist "political correctness" lie as much in the economic interests of the academy as they do in the political predilections of the faculty.

Political Influence on Science

As an example, I draw attention to my field of expertise, which is climate change science and policy. The Environmental Protection Agency [EPA] claims to base its global warming regulations on "sound" science, in which the federal government is virtually the sole provider of research funding. In fact, climate change science and policy is a highly charged political arena, and its $2 billion/year public funding would not exist save for the perception that global warming is very high on the nation's priority list.

The universities and their federal funders have evolved a codependent relationship. Again, let's use climate change as an example. Academic scientists recognize that only the federal government provides the significant funds necessary to publish enough original research to gain tenure in the higher levels of academia. Their careers therefore depend on it. Meanwhile, the political support for elected officials who hope to gain from global warming science will go away if science dismisses the issue as unimportant.

The culture of exaggeration and the disincentives to minimize scientific/policy problems are an unintended consequence of the way we now do science, which is itself a direct descendant of *Science: The Endless Frontier*.

All the disciplines of science with policy implications (and this is by far most of them) compete with each other for finite budgetary resources, resources that are often allocated via various congressional committees, such as those charged with responsibilities for environmental science, technology, or medical research. Thus, each of the constituent research communities must engage in demonstrations that *their* scientific purview is more important to society than those of their colleagues in other disciplines. So, using this example, global warming inadvertently competes with cancer research and others.

How Scientific Issues Get Exaggerated

Imagine if a NASA [National Aeronautics and Space Administration] administrator at a congressional hearing, upon being asked if global warming were of sufficient importance to justify a billion dollars in additional funding, replied that it really was an exaggerated issue, and the money should be spent elsewhere on more important problems.

It is a virtual certainty that such a reply would be one of his last acts as administrator.

So, at the end of this hypothetical hearing, having answered in the affirmative (perhaps more like, "hell yes, we can use the money"), the administrator gathers all of his department heads and demands programmatic proposals from each. Will any one of these individuals submit one which states that his department really doesn't want the funding because the issue is perhaps exaggerated?

It is a virtual certainty that such a reply would be one of his last acts as a department head.

The department heads now turn to their individual scientists, asking for specific proposals on how to put the new monies to use. Who will submit a proposal with the working research hypothesis that climate change isn't all that important?

It is a virtual certainty that such a reply would guarantee he was in his last year as a NASA scientist.

Now that the funding has been established and disbursed, the research is performed under the obviously supported hypotheses (which may largely be stated as "it's worse than we thought"). When the results are submitted to a peer-reviewed journal, they are going to be reviewed by other scientists who, being prominent in the field of climate change by virtue of their research productivity, are funded by the same process. They have little incentive to block any papers consistent with the worsening hypothesis and every incentive to block one that concludes the opposite.

Determining That Bias Exists

Can this really be true? After all, what I have sketched here is simply a hypothesis that public choice is fostering a pervasive

"it's worse than we thought" bias in the climate science literature, with the attendant policy distortions that must result
from relying upon that literature.

It is an hypothesis that tests easily.

Let us turn to a less highly charged field in applied science
to determine how to test the hypothesis of pervasive bias,
namely the pedestrian venue of the daily weather forecast.

Short-range weather models and centennial-scale climate
models are largely based upon the same physics derived from
the six interacting "primitive equations" describing atmospheric motion and thermodynamics. The difference is that,
in the weather forecasting models, the initial conditions
change, being a simultaneous sample of global atmospheric
pressure, temperature, and moisture in three dimensions,
measured by ascending weather balloons and, increasingly, by
downward-sounding satellites. This takes place twice a day.
The "boundary conditions," such as solar irradiance and the
transfer of radiation through the atmosphere, do not change.
In a climate model, the base variables are calculated, rather
than measured, and the boundary conditions—such as the absorption of infrared radiation in various layers of the atmosphere (the "greenhouse effect") change over time.

It is assumed that the weather forecasting model is unbiased—without remaining systematic errors—so that each run,
every twelve hours, has an equal probability of predicting, say,
that it will be warmer or colder next Friday than the previous
run. If this were not the case, then the chance of warmer or
colder is unequal. In fact, in the developmental process for
forecast models, the biases are subtracted out and the output
is forced to have a bias of zero and therefore an equal probability of a warmer or colder forecast.

Similarly, if the initial results are unbiased, successive runs
of climate models should have an equal probability of producing centennial forecasts that are warmer or colder than the
previous one, or projecting more or less severe climate im-

pacts. It is a fact that the climate change calculated by these models is *not a* change from current or past conditions, but is the product of subtracting the output of the model with low greenhouse gas concentrations from the one with higher ones. Consequently the biasing errors have been subtracted out, a rather intriguing trick. Again, the change is one model minus another, not the standard "predicted minus observed."

The Evidence of Bias

The climate research community actually believes its models are zero biased. An *amicus* brief in the landmark Supreme Court case *Massachusetts v. EPA* [Environmental Protection Agency], by a number of climate scientists claiming to speak for the larger community, explicitly stated this as fact: "Outcomes may turn out better than our best current prediction, but it is just as possible that environmental and health damages will be more severe than best predictions. . . ."

The operative words are "just as possible," indicating that climate scientists believe they are immune to public choice influences.

This is testable, and I ran such a test, publishing it in an obscure journal, *Energy & Environment*, in 2008. I, perhaps accurately, hypothesized that a paper severely criticizing the editorial process at *Science* and *Nature*, the two most prestigious general science journals worldwide, was not likely to be published in such prominent places.

I examined the 115 articles that had appeared in both of these journals during a 13-month period in 2006 and 2007, classifying them as either "worse than we thought," "better," or "neutral or cannot determine." 23 were neutral and removed from consideration. 9 were "better" and 83 were "worse." Because of the hypothesis of nonbiased equiprobability, this is equivalent to tossing a coin 92 times and coming up with 9 or fewer heads or tails. The probability that this would occur in an unbiased sample can be calculated from the binomial probability distribution, and the result is striking. There would have to be 100,000,000,000,000,000 iterations of the 92 tosses for there to be merely a 50% chance that one realization of 9 or fewer heads or tails would be observed.

In subsequent work, I recently assembled a much larger sample of the scientific literature and, while the manuscript is in preparation, I can state that my initial result appears to be robust.

Kealey tells us that there is no relationship between the wealth of nations and the amount of money that taxpayers spend on scientific research. In reality, it is in fact "worse than he thought." At least in a highly politicized field such as global warming science and policy, the more money the public spends, the worse is the quality of the science.

"As government scientific funding tapers down, our students and professional researchers increasingly lack the tools and supplies they need for their work."

Cuts in Government Funding for Science Research Endanger the National Economy

David Eisenberg

In the following viewpoint, David Eisenberg explains that government funding of scientific research is decreasing and that without it scientists will not have the lab equipment their work requires. Even experienced and highly regarded scientists are losing their grants, he says, and fear of funding loss is causing faculty members to cut back on the number of students and employees in their labs. In his opinion, the resulting decline in scientific discoveries will cause America to be surpassed by the rest of the world and will damage the US economy. Eisenberg is a professor at the University of California, Los Angeles (UCLA) medical school and the director of the UCLA-DOE (US Department of Energy) Institute for Genomics and Proteomics.

As you read, consider the following questions:

1. What are the sources of funding for scientific research at UCLA, according to the viewpoint?

2. According to Eisenberg, what effect did the federal government shutdown of October 2013 have on scientific research?

3. How, in Eisenberg's opinion, do increases in red tape damage scientific research?

Classes and instruction go on as usual at UCLA [the University of California, Los Angeles], but those of us dedicated also to scientific research are increasingly squeezed by the United States budget sequestration [across-the-board reduction of government spending] and the federal government shutdown [of October 2013].

The dollars that pay for most of the work in our labs come from the federal government. True, the University of California supports most faculty salaries, and some private foundations such as the Howard Hughes Medical Institute support university research, but the great bulk of UCLA research funding comes from the National Institutes of Health, the National Science Foundation and the U.S. Department of Energy.

Without these funds from U.S. government agencies, there would be almost no scientific equipment in our labs. We would be paralyzed without expensive supplies such as chemicals and enzymes and we would be unable to provide salary support for the scientists who carry out the day-to-day research. These scientists include the graduate research assistants who are learning how to do research as well as postdoctoral fellows and professional scientists.

As government scientific funding tapers down, our students and professional researchers increasingly lack the tools and supplies they need for their work, and we are faced more and more often with the unpleasant task of telling our colleagues that we can no longer support them.

On the larger scale, the stream of scientific discoveries that has created and fueled our biotechnology, information technology and green energy economy is drying up. To the extent that this stream dwindles, America surrenders new technologies to the rest of the world and our economy is sure to wind down, too.

The research budgets of the National Institutes of Health and the Department of Energy have not kept pace with the number of U.S. scientists over the past several years. Stretched thin already, the budgets of these agencies have been cut anew by the budget sequestration. I hear every day of California scientists who have lost funding for their labs. Even one of the new California Nobel Prize awardees in chemistry recently reported on National Public Radio that he had lost the research grant that had supported his work for 20 years.

The federal government shutdown is further dragging us down.

Submission of new grant proposals has been suspended, and the peer review system which prioritizes the few grants available for funding has now ground to a halt.

From the National Institutes of Health, no new grants are now being awarded. Also, government-run websites, such as those of the National Library of Medicine, essential for our work, are faltering. In addition, government-supported research facilities, such as the crucial synchrotron particle accelerators, may have to close. Fear of funding loss is causing UCLA faculty to cut back on the number of students and employees in their labs.

Further Burdens on American Science

Loss of indirect funding, which comes to the campus as a percentage of all awarded research grants, is also falling. That is, when we scientists receive grants, a percentage of the funds do

Cutting of Funds Leads to "Brain Drain"

The problem, Professor Tom Antonsen said, was not just how the lack of funding would impact graybeards like himself, but also the newcomers to the field. Young scientists who had spent 12 years studying for their PhDs would find the climate inhospitable, and future generations would look elsewhere.

"We used to be able to tell people that there was some kind of job security," he said. "That would be a compensation for not being paid as much. Now, if you are taking a big risk in investing 12 years of your life to learn how to do the science, people will think twice."

The nontechnical term for this is "brain drain." It had been happening for years prior to sequestration, though the recent cuts have accelerated it. Antonsen, a plasma physicist who studies the production and interaction of electromagnetic fields with matter, said he has lost two staffers so far: One has left the country and another accepted a job at a Wall Street bank. A third is currently looking for work outside the field.

[Professor Anindya] Dutta said a prospective hire in India had recently turned down a job offer in favor of going to Germany.

"That was unheard of not too long ago," he said.

Sam Stein, "Sequestration Ushers in a Dark Age for Science in America," Huffington Post, *August 14, 2013.*

not go to our labs, but instead to the UCLA administration. These indirect funds are supposed to pay for the upkeep of our buildings and campus services, such as fund management and personnel management.

As a consequence, janitorial services have been cut back, worsening conditions in our labs, many of which are decades old, having enjoyed no renovations. While funding is diminishing, red tape increasingly entangles us. Some new safety requirements are onerous without truly increasing safety, making students cynical. Each month brings new forms for us to fill out, devouring time and threatening to freeze the former dynamism of American science.

Imagine my surprise last month [in September 2013] when I visited the University of Leuven, located in a Belgian city with a population of less than 100,000 people.

There I saw spacious modern laboratories, a striking contrast to some of our shabby research spaces. Students and postdoctoral fellows there are well supported. Their productivity is excellent and I heard few complaints from lab leaders about funding, which is abundant and reliable.

Meanwhile Congress dithers, endangering the vitality of American science and, by extension, our economy.

> "No evidence shows that government bureaucrats have either the qualifications or the incentives to make better decisions than private individuals and organizations about what research should be funded."

Government Funding of Medical Research Injects Politics into Scientific Questions

Michael D. Tanner

In the following viewpoint, Michael D. Tanner argues that although government funding of medical research is supported by most voters, it should receive the same scrutiny as other programs and that it is neither worth the cost nor necessary to supplement private funding. Also, Tanner points out that government funding of science means that the research will be influenced by political issues and that it may hinder scientific advancement by making scientists unwilling to challenge the current consensus. Tanner is a senior fellow at the Cato Institute.

As you read, consider the following questions:

1. By what means, according to Tanner, have some politicians proposed getting more government funds for medical research?

2. According to Tanner, what percentage of medical research is privately funded?

3. Why, in Tanner's opinion, does private funding of research avoid moral and philosophical questions that arise with controversial government funding?

Few government programs seem as sacrosanct as funding for medical research. Despite continuing budget constraints, both Democrats and Republicans regularly pledge to increase funding for the National Institutes of Health [NIH] and other government medical research.

This week, Eric Cantor of Virginia, the second-ranking House Republican, called for continued government funding for such research. "There is an appropriate and necessary role for the federal government to ensure funding for basic medical research," Cantor declared, suggesting that federal funds used for social science research should be shifted to medical programs instead.

Polls show that a strong majority of U.S. voters support funding medical research. Yet there is no reason that it shouldn't receive the same critical scrutiny as any other federal program.

First, are the benefits worth the cost? Terence Kealey, vice chancellor of the University of Buckingham in England and author of *The Economic Laws of Scientific Research*, says that a review of historical evidence shows little correlation between the amount of money governments spend on scientific research and the returns from such investment. Kealey studied the full range of scientific research, including medical research.

The Debate Over Science Policy Is Mainly About Money

No political party is immune from exacerbating distortions created by politicized science, as politicians channel federal dollars back home regardless of scientific merit. In a sense, the debate over science policy and where to allocate taxpayer resources isn't one over science policy as such; rather, it's over problems of allocating the spoils artificially created when government (an institution with the power to tax) gets involved in the very production of knowledge itself (and seducing industry), rather than in merely protecting rights in the property that knowledge makes possible. . . .

Disconnecting science from the technological gains to mankind in the name of "basic" research can become a misguided passion. Science is likely to advance human welfare and remain most relevant to mankind if it is pulled into being by the actual needs of humanity, including practical ones.

Wayne Crews, Testimony Before the House of Representatives Committee on Science, Space, and Technology, March 17, 2010.

Second, there is no proof that the private sector is incapable of financing medical research, either for profit or as charity. While private companies undoubtedly have an incentive to fund research that they believe will ultimately prove profitable, even "orphan" drugs—one of the least profitable lines of research, as they are designed for a small number of people with rare disorders—have found funding through the Bill and Melinda Gates Foundation and other charities.

Currently 60 percent to 70 percent of medical research is privately paid for, but research from the Paris-based Organisation for Economic Co-operation and Development suggests that if private companies believe governments will pay for research, they may simply withdraw their own money. Thus, government funding doesn't result in more research, just a different funding stream.

Politics Undermines Research

No evidence shows that government bureaucrats have either the qualifications or the incentives to make better decisions than private individuals and organizations about what research should be funded. After all, government involvement in research inevitably injects politics into scientific questions. Even former National Institutes of Health director Elias Zerhouni has warned that congressional mandates to spend money on specific diseases have undermined the agencies' research. And Cantor's statement itself suggested the politicization of government research through his desire to transfer funds from research that he doesn't like (social science) to research that he favors (medical).

Similarly, researchers are far more likely to receive government grants if they belong to the scientific "club," a good-old-boys network of researchers. Some researchers worry they can have their grants cut for challenging the scientific consensus or for reaching conclusions that are politically controversial. This is dangerous, because a willingness to rethink current theories is a key to scientific advancement.

Moreover, government funding of medical research inevitably entangles the government in difficult social issues. Recall the bitter debate over government funding for stem cell research. Other issues that have stirred up recent political controversy include the use of animals for testing, Centers for Disease Control and Prevention research into gun violence, and NIH research on sexual practices. We even saw President Barack Obama's choice for NIH director, Francis Collins, attacked for being an evangelical Christian.

Private funding avoids such moral and philosophical quandaries by allowing individual donors or corporate shareholders to exercise their personal consciences.

An industrial policy for medical research is still an industrial policy—and likely to have the same inefficiencies and unintended consequences. Or as Kealey put it, "Scientists may love government money, and politicians may love the power its expenditure confers upon them, but society is impoverished by the transaction."

> *"If a lot of money is available one year and none the next, it creates an extremely unstable environment, . . . and the country loses more money in the long run due to inefficiency."*

Government Research Funding Is Essential for Maintaining World Leadership in Science

Alexander Nakhnikian

In the following viewpoint, Alexander Nakhnikian discusses the devastating effect of recent cuts in federal funding on scientific research. He points out that operating modern laboratories is extremely costly and that the goals of private firms are not always compatible with good science. He argues that politicians' allocation of funds for science varies from year to year on the basis of what they think will get them the most votes, often causing projects on which millions of dollars have been spent to be terminated before the scientists have a chance to produce results. In his opinion, more stable funding is essential to maintaining America's role as a world leader in scientific development. Nakhnikian is a doctoral candidate in neuroscience and cognitive science at Indiana University.

Alexander Nakhnikian, "Cutting Off Our Nose to Spite Our Face: Scientific Funding in the Age of Sequestration," *Violent Metaphors* (blog), September 1, 2013. violentmetaphors.com. Copyright © 2013 by Alexander Nakhnikian. All rights reserved. Reproduced with permission.

As you read, consider the following questions:

1. According to Nakhnikian, what does the government do to counteract the bias bound to occur in research done by drug companies?

2. According to Nakhnikian, what is the minimum time normally needed to conduct an important series of experiments in the biological sciences?

3. Why, as explained by Nakhnikian, does the scientific community not save money when it has extra funds to use when funding is insufficient?

Science is important. Really, really important. Most Americans agree about this. Unfortunately, we don't always act as though scientific progress is a high priority. That's partly because of the American love/hate relationship with science as a way of viewing the world, which is most evident in the fights over creationism, climate change, and vaccination. But there's another factor in play that often gets overlooked because it seems so mundane: Money. We need it. Lots of it. And these days, we don't have it.

Running a modern, cutting-edge lab is like running a small business. It takes hundreds of thousands, if not millions, of dollars a year to pay employees, maintain facilities, and afford the equipment required to conduct research. But unlike most small businesses, most labs doing basic research aren't turning a profit. Instead, they do work that may lead to big breakthroughs in scientific knowledge—and, ultimately, big profits for drug companies and others.

To give an example from my field, neurodegenerative disorders such as Parkinson's disease can be studied at either a foundational or a profit-driven level. At the profit-driven level, you have the search for new drugs and surgical devices that can improve a patient's symptoms. But these would not be possible were it not for basic research that was funded by foundations. L-DOPA, the premier drug for treating Parkinson's disease, is a result of painstaking, years-long research into complex chemical pathways in the brain that culminated in the development of a new drug. Nobody made millions of dollars discovering one more little detail about how the brain makes dopamine, the chemical that is deficient in Parkinson's patients, but without that work, the drug companies' money-making, lifesaving innovations would have had no foundation upon which to build.

The fact is that the flow of capital in a purely market-based system is not optimal for some kinds of work, and scientific research is one of them. Moreover, private firms often have goals that are at odds with the goals of good science. If a particular drug is a danger to the public, we're not going to find out if all the funding for drug research comes from the drug companies. To work around this problem, the government subsidizes basic research through organizations such as the National Science Foundation (NSF) and the National Institutes of Health (NIH). These organizations account for a tiny sliver of the national budget, yet the return on the investment is huge. There are few uses of taxpayer dollars that result in more direct benefits for the economy, the nation, and the American public.

Long Term vs. Short term

But science operates on long timescales, and politics does not. Completing a sound series of experiments in the biological sciences, something that will really advance science and medicine, takes at least five years, if not ten or twenty. Politicians, on the other hand, are generally focused on the short term, touting whatever they think will get them more votes. If one year they want to appear "serious about science" they might up NIH's budget 10%, but if in the next year they want to appear "serious about the debt" they might cut the budget by 5%—which is actually an even bigger hit when you factor in inflation. It's not the best way of doing business, but the research community has thrived in spite of these difficulties for decades. This is no longer the case.

The recent economic collapse and the sequester [across-the-board reduction of government spending] have bled us dry. [Political journalist] Sam Stein, writing for the *Huffington Post*, has produced an excellent series on the impact that the sequester has had on individual scientists. Not only are we losing the chance to fund new projects, we are prematurely terminating ongoing projects that have already cost millions of dollars. This makes about as much sense as filling up the tank, then setting your car on fire because you don't want to bother changing the oil.

In an attempt to refute Mr. Stein, the *Washington Examiner* ran an op-ed claiming, more or less, that Mr. Stein is exaggerating and that scientists are just a bunch of whiners. The *Examiner* points out that NIH's funding is actually higher now than it was under either [President George W.] Bush or [President Bill] Clinton. How then could we be living through such hard times?

It is technically true that NIH's funding went up, and it makes sense at face value that if more money is available we should be fine. But this line of thinking simply doesn't match up with the facts on the ground. I won't go into details about the things we've done to save money in our field, but I will say one of my advisors was literally dodging bullets a few years back because of the need to stay in a cheap hotel while attending a neuroscience conference—and that was before the sequester hit.

When I read the *Examiner's* op-ed, I remembered something I tell my stats students: The main reason to take stats is not to learn math, it's to become very good at recognizing when an argument is full of horse excrement. Let's put that skill to use. Just looking at the raw numbers is never a good idea; it is necessary to dig a little deeper.

An Unstable Budget

The doubling of NIH's budget is accounted for almost entirely by a series of large increases from the late 90s to the early 2000s, when times were good and President Bush wanted to deflect criticism of his administration's handling of science. (Long story short, [Vice President] Dick Cheney strong-armed Congress to cut funding that was already allocated for medical research because one of the aims was to test the effects of condoms on the spread of HIV. This offended members of the administration's political base, who saw it as an attack on abstinence only sex education.) After that, things started to go south and funding slowed down so much that it no longer matched inflation. At the same time, NIH became committed to spending the money it had, since there's no point just sitting on funds that could be going to productive research. The problem is that, once a project is funded, you're on the hook for at least 5 years, which means that drastic cuts during that time will have a devastating effect on the new research. Those annual increases, though small, sounded big because a little chunk of 25 billion is a lot more than a little chunk of 19 billion. But the total amount matters less than how stable things are from one year to another. And between the fact that NIH is awarding fewer inflation-adjusted dollars per year and the fact that there are so many more projects to be funded, the net result is that hundreds/thousands of scientists are left wondering if they'll have to abandon their research before it is done.

The need to cut ongoing projects would be less troubling if we were simply defunding projects that yielded few valuable results, but this is not the case. Stein's recent posts are a good source of information on the sorts of projects that are being cut. We are defunding promising research that would have surely received continued funding ten years ago. My own discussions with professors who have recently reviewed grants for NIH paint a very bleak picture. The consensus is that there are too many worthy projects and too few dollars to fund them. Grants that would have been funded without a second thought during other years are reluctantly denied due to the budget.

Here's another way of looking at things. Congress threw a bunch of money at us every year for a while, and because that money is still officially part of the NIH budget, it looks as though things aren't so bad. However, that money has, in effect, already been spent, so there is not enough to fund all the projects that were started before annual increases stopped keeping up with inflation. I cannot overstate the importance of ongoing funding. For a research group to lose a grant because they failed to demonstrate the utility of their work is one thing. In the present situation, however, labs that are producing novel, useful results are considering whether to shut down due to lack of funds.

It might be tempting to ask why the scientific community didn't sit on its extra funds for a "rainy day." The short answer is "that's not how it works." If NIH did withhold funds in case things get bad, Congress would likely cut funding even further, while asking "why the heck aren't you using the money we already gave you?" And, since there are always good research ideas in need of funding, it's not hard to find worthy projects if you have grants to give out.

The Need for New Funds

Besides, it's not enough just to fund established projects. Research is a twofold process: We need dedicated funding to maintain ongoing projects, and we need liquid assets to be allocated to new research. Each year new PhDs start trying to set up their own labs. We need new funds available for start-up money. That is *not* to say that we need huge budget increases each year. However, if a lot of money is available one year and none the next, it creates an extremely unstable environment in which research is stymied, careers are damaged, and the country loses more money in the long run due to inefficiency.

The sequester just demonstrates, through an extreme case, how disastrous the effects of sudden and heavy budget cuts can be for the sciences. Granted, the economy is a mess across the board right now, but cutting funding for research is, frankly, one of the stupidest things we can do to fix the debt. Federal funding for science is such a small part of the budget, and it provides so much bang for the buck, that trying to fix the debt by cutting research funding is like trying to lose weight by cutting off your thumbs.

Healing the system is crucial to maintaining our role as a world leader in scientific development. As a professional scientist I wish to see my field move forward, and as an American I have no desire to surrender our place as the nexus of major advances in science and technology. Our first priority must be undoing the immediate effects of the sequester. After that, advocacy for a more stable, more predictable policy regarding scientific funding will go a long way toward improving our productivity, our place in the world, and the well-being of the public.

The scientific community cannot do this on our own. We need the help of engaged, informed citizens who recognize the hard work it will take to rebuild the foundations of American research, and who realize that this is a fight worth joining.

Periodical and Internet Sources Bibliography

The following articles have been selected to supplement the diverse views presented in this chapter.

William J. Broad	"Billionaires with Big Ideas Are Privatizing American Science," *New York Times*, March 15, 2014.
Hank Campbell	"2 Dirty Secrets About Science Funding," *Science 2.0*, November 6, 2013.
Eric Cantor and Lamar Smith	"Rethinking Science Funding," *USA Today*, September 30, 2013.
Michael Helms	"Why I Support Corporate Funding of Research," *Technician Online*, October 25, 2013.
Rachael Jolley	"Cuts and Shutdowns Are Hurting Science," *Slate*, April 20, 2014.
Terence Kealey	"The Case Against Public Science," *Cato Unbound*, August 5, 2013.
Henry I. Miller	"A Lot of Good Research Doesn't Get Funded, So Why Are We Wasting Money on Junk?," *Forbes*, February 12, 2014.
Sam Stein	"Sequestration Ushers in a Dark Age for Science in America," *Huffington Post*, August 14, 2013.
Michael Stratford	"Moving Beyond Congress," *Inside Higher Ed*, October 11, 2013.
Liz Szabo	"NIH Director: Budget Cuts Put U.S. Science at Risk," *USA Today*, April 23, 2014.
Dan Vergano	"Coalition Issues SOS! (Save Our Science Funding)," *USA Today*, May 4, 2013.

CHAPTER 2

Is There Too Much Regulation of Scientific Research?

Chapter Preface

One of the most familiar ways in which scientific research is regulated is through the requirement that no research on human subjects—whether medical, psychological, or social—may be done without official approval. This rule was established because in the mid-twentieth century, several unethical experiments were performed that aroused a public outcry when they came to light; for example, in the infamous government-run Tuskegee syphilis study, black men with the disease were not treated with penicillin because researchers wanted to study untreated patients. The federal Department of Health and Human Services then decided that all human-subject research, even if privately funded, should be reviewed before it is undertaken.

The review is done by bodies called institutional review boards (IRBs), formed at universities and other research institutions, which judge proposed research according to standards set forth by the government. Although no federal law mandates this, it is a requirement for obtaining government funds, not only for the research involved but also for all research done at the institution. Moreover, many state laws require it. Thus, there is no way to do any kind of research involving humans unless it has been approved by an IRB.

This is an important safeguard; no one wants people to be harmed for the sake of science or subjected to risky experimentation without their informed consent. However, some researchers feel it has been carried too far. It covers not only potentially harmful experiments and significant invasions of privacy but also trivial matters such as asking subjects to fill out anonymous questionnaires. It is costly, as there are fees for review by IRBs, and a study may involve subjects at multiple locations. The decisions of an IRB may be influenced by the biases of its members, and it is a slow process.

Ben Goldacre, writing in the British newspaper the *Guardian* about a similar ethical review system in the United Kingdom, describes a case in which doctors wanted to compare two treatments for serious head injury. To get scientifically valid results, they had to conduct a formal study instead of just looking at the benefit to individual patients, and this required authorization by the board. "It was a famously hard-fought battle with ethics committees, even though both treatments—steroids, or no steroids—were in widespread, routine use," Goldacre writes. "Finally, when approval was granted, it turned out that steroids were killing patients. Only a trial could give us this information. Head injury is common. Patients died unnecessarily while we waited for this trial to be approved."

A more fundamental objection to the review system is that some scholars believe it is unconstitutional. In the July 1, 2013, issue of *Commentary*, Columbia Law School professor Philip Hamburger writes, "These 'IRBs' have suppressed vast amounts of talking, printing, and publishing—even mere reading and analyzing—for hundreds of thousands of Americans. This is utterly unconstitutional, and in stifling research and its publication, it has proved deadly.... Some review boards actually order scholars and students to stop analyzing data." Therefore, he points out, "review boards not only license the acquisition and publication of information; they not only require the destruction of knowledge; they also bar thinking."

There are many other ways in which scientific research is regulated by the government. The authors in this chapter debate whether there is too much regulation of scientific research.

> *"Compliance requirements are taking researchers out of the laboratory and reducing their ability to perform the research that leads to the innovations that improve our quality of life."*

Excessive Federal Regulation Diverts Scientists' Time from Research

Tobin L. Smith, Josh Trapani, Anthony DeCrappeo, and David Kennedy

In the following viewpoint, Tobin L. Smith, Josh Trapani, Anthony DeCrappeo, and David Kennedy explain how excessive regulation is decreasing the morale of scientists, taking time away from their research, and adding significantly to the cost of the research. They point out areas in which it is unreasonable to apply government regulations designed for industry to universities, among them reporting of time devoted to specific activities, antiterrorism standards for chemical laboratories, and paperwork required for foreign workers. Universities should be exempted from many such regulations, they say, or if not exempted, they should be reimbursed for the cost of complying with such

Tobin L. Smith, Josh Trapani, Anthony DeCrappeo, and David Kennedy, "Reforming Regulation of Research Universities," *Issues in Science and Technology*, Summer 2011, reissued November 27, 2013. www.issues.org. Copyright © 2013 by Tobin L. Smith. All rights reserved. Reproduced with permission.

rules. Tobin L. Smith is vice president for policy and Josh Tra-
pani is senior policy analyst at the Association of American Uni-
versities in Washington, DC. Anthony DeCrappeo is president
and David Kennedy is director of costing policies at the Council
on Governmental Relations in Washington, DC.

As you read, consider the following questions:

1. According to the example given by the authors, how
   much has the cost of complying with regulations at a
   prominent medical school increased during the first decade of this century?

2. Why, according to the viewpoint, could the
   government's requirements for detailed effort reporting
   by universities be eliminated without affecting its oversight of their research?

3. What change do the authors suggest making to regulations concerned with the risk in experiments?

In recent years, research universities and their faculty have
seen a steady stream of new federal regulations and reporting requirements imposed on them. These new requirements,
in combination with other factors, have exacerbated already
significant institutional financial stress and diverted faculty
time from research and education.

The oversight of research that uses human subjects or animals, involves select agents, chemicals, or other potentially
dangerous substances, or involves export-controlled technologies is necessary and important. Universities and researchers
take seriously their responsibilities to comply with requirements and account for their use of federal resources. However,
increasing regulatory and reporting requirements are not only
costly in monetary terms; they also reduce faculty productivity
and result in inefficient use of federal research dollars.

Quantifying the monetary and productivity costs of regulations is often difficult. Whereas the cost of each individual

regulation may not appear to be significant, the real problem is the gradual, ever-increasing growth or stacking of regulations.

The fiscal situation of our universities requires a reexamination of regulatory and reporting requirements to ensure a proper balance between accountability and risk management and to ensure that federal and institutional resources, as well as researchers' time and effort, are being used effectively and efficiently. . . .

Universities Deserve Attention

Higher education has largely been absent from recent governmental discussions of regulatory reform, despite evidence contained in a report prepared for the U.S. Commission on the Future of Higher Education that "there may already be more federal regulation of higher education than in most other industries." As documented by Catholic University of America's Office of General Counsel, more than 200 federal statutes affect higher education, and the list keeps growing. Sen. Lamar Alexander (R-TN) recognized this when he asked the National Research Council's (NRC's) Committee on Research Universities, at their November 2010 meeting, to identify ways to improve the health of U.S. research universities that would not cost the federal government money, pointing specifically at the problem of overregulation. . . .

At the same time that other funding sources have become constrained, the cost of performing research has become increasingly expensive for universities, in part because of the expanded costs of federal compliance. . . .

Heavy compliance burdens affect not only institutions, but also the morale and productivity of researchers within them. According to an often-cited and illustrative figure from the 2007 Federal Demonstration Partnership (FDP) Faculty Burden Survey, 42% of faculty time relating to the conduct of federally funded research is spent on administrative duties.

Some of this additional time is the result of increased activities relating to compliance with federal regulations. In effect, at a time of limited resources, compliance requirements are taking researchers out of the laboratory and reducing their ability to perform the research that leads to the innovations that improve our quality of life. . . .

Most of the research compliance costs are accumulated in a pool of costs classified by OMB [Office of Management and Budget] as "sponsored projects administration" (SPA), and analysis of SPA can be insightful in measuring the growth of research compliance costs. One private institution in the Midwest estimated that its SPA costs increased from $4.2 million in 2002 to $7.3 million in 2008. A prominent medical school in the Southeast reported that its compliance and quality assurance costs increased from about $3 million in 2000 to $12.5 million in 2010.

More telling than the increases in SPA and associated research compliance costs are trends showing that these costs have increased more rapidly than the associated direct research expenditures, such as salaries, lab supplies, and research equipment. . . .

It is important to note that this is not a case of administrative inefficiency. University-wide administration and department and school-specific academic administration rates have fallen over the past decade, due mainly to drastic cuts in state appropriations and a strong emphasis on administrative efficiency and effective management. At the same time, SPA costs, which are closely linked to the cost of research compliance, have increased. The onslaught of research compliance regulation and unfunded mandates has overwhelmed the strong downward pressures of budget cuts and emphasis on administrative efficiency.

Precisely answering the seemingly simple question "How much does it cost universities to comply with any particular regulation?" is difficult. The cost of compliance frequently results from the time that faculty, staff, and administrators spend in fulfilling compliance and reporting responsibilities. This results in both monetary costs and the diversion of faculty time away from research and teaching, reducing productivity. . . .

A Framework for Evaluation and Solutions

Although the ever-growing array of research regulations affecting universities can seem bewildering, solutions for problematic regulations fit within a relatively small number of categories:

- Eliminate outright or exempt universities from the regulation

- Harmonize the regulation across agencies to avoid duplication and redundancy

- Tier the regulation to levels of risk rather than assuming that one size fits all

- Refocus the regulation on performance-based goals rather than on process

- Adjust the regulation to better fit the academic research environment. . . .

Effort Reporting

Effort reports show the percentage of total effort that individuals contribute to university activities. Faculty commit to devote a certain fraction of their work time to specific projects funded by the federal government, and must regularly certify that they are devoting this amount of time to those activities. . . .

Effort reporting can be eliminated without any detriment to the accountability or oversight of the research enterprise for five reasons. First, it is redundant. Requirements that faculty provide regular progress reports to funding agencies serve the same function as effort reporting, but do so more effectively because they better align with incentives for faculty performance such as research accomplishments, success on subsequent grant proposals, and ultimately promotion and tenure. Second, it is unnecessary. Faculty rarely spend less time than they initially commit to federally funded research. Indeed, as acknowledged by the OMB A-21 Clarification Memo of January 2001, faculty routinely spend more time than they committed to. Third, it lacks precision. It is incompatible with an academic research environment in which researchers do not work on billable hours and researcher responsibilities such as student supervision often cannot realistically be billed reliably to a single project. Fourth, it is expensive and wasteful of government funds. The federal government must spend money in the auditing of effort reports and associated administrative processes. Finally, effort reporting is responsible for adding considerably to universities' administrative costs and taking faculty away from research. Virtually every institution that responded to our request for information identified effort reporting as an area that has had significant cost and productivity implications.

The costs are significant. For example, one public university in the Midwest told us that nine employees spend about one-quarter of their time each year monitoring certifications, at an estimated annual cost of $117,000. For many schools, effort reporting also requires the development or purchase and the continuing maintenance of specialized software systems. A public university in the Midwest reported that the cost of the necessary software was more than $500,000, exclusive of implementation and training costs. Several universities reported that they spent in the range of $500,000 to $1 million annually on effort reporting.

Chemical Facility Anti-Terrorism Standards

The Department of Homeland Security (DHS) Appropriations Act of 2007 granted DHS the authority to regulate chemical facilities that present "high levels of security risk." Under this authority, DHS promulgated CFATS [Chemical Facility Anti-Terrorism Standards]. Since 2007, the research community has urged DHS to reconsider the manner in which CFATS is applied to research laboratories located at universities.

The current regulations fail to recognize the differences between university research laboratories and major chemical manufacturing and production facilities, including how chemicals are used and stored for research purposes. Chemical plants often store large volumes of toxic substances; universities generally do not. Rather, they distribute regulated "chemicals of interest" in very small quantities, among laboratories in multiple buildings and generally in more than one geographic location. Given this distributed environment, research organizations present a low risk for serious toxic releases through theft, sabotage, or attack. . . .

DHS should take an approach in which the security requirements apply only to individual laboratories where chemicals of interest exist in quantities greater than the threshold planning quantity.

U.S. Citizenship and Immigration Services Changes

In early 2011, the U.S. Citizenship and Immigration Services (USCIS) added a question about export control licenses to its Form I-129, which employers must complete when petitioning for a foreign worker to come to the United States temporarily to perform services. As a result, I-129 petitioners now have to complete a new certification for H-1B visas and certain other specialty occupation visa petitions. This new requirement puts substantial burdens on universities with questionable benefit for national security. . . .

Most research conducted by foreign nationals at U.S. research universities is fundamental research, which is excluded from export control requirements. Whether technology is sub-

Freedom of Scientific Inquiry Is Not Guaranteed by the Constitution

Many Americans would likely attribute the success of science in this country to the freedom of inquiry it has traditionally enjoyed, a concept similar to those of political and religious freedom enshrined in our Constitution. It may therefore come as a surprise to many that, unlike the latter two freedoms which are guaranteed by express provisions of the Constitution, scientific freedom has no comparable guarantee. The closest the Constitution comes to protecting scientific freedom are the First Amendment's guarantees of freedom of "speech" and the "press." Hence the issue of whether scientists can claim constitutional protection against allegedly unreasonable intrusions by the government into the domain of scientific research is a looming and unsettled question in American law.

Barry McDonald,
"Government Regulation or Other 'Abridgements' of
Scientific Research," Emory Law Journal, *vol. 54, no. 2, 2005.*

ject to Export Administration Regulations is irrelevant if a foreign national is performing fundamental research. Because of this exclusion, there will probably be very few instances in which export-control licenses will be required for foreign nationals employed at research universities on H-1B visas. However, universities must do significant additional review for I-129 submissions to confirm that this is indeed the case. . . .

It is also unrealistic in a research environment to expect that export-control issues and technologies connected to a particular line of research in which a researcher is involved will remain static from the time Form I-129 is completed.

Universities cannot predict where scientific inquiry will go, and many technologies involved in conducting research may change during the course of the research project as findings and discoveries progress. It is thus easy for universities to inadvertently respond to this question in a way that could eventually turn out to be inaccurate. . . .

Other Examples

Other examples involve tiering regulations to risk. In human subject research, minimal-risk studies, such as many in the social sciences, should not require the same level of review as clinical trials. Similarly, not all research involving pathogens or biological toxins that pose potential risks to public health and safety pose the same level of risk. The requirements associated with the regulation of this "select agents" research should be tiered to risk, as documented by the American Society of Microbiology.

And finally, newly proposed conflict of interest guidelines from NIH [National Institutes of Health] that require public posting of faculty-industry relationships, even when potential conflicts are being effectively managed, will create public confusion and unnecessary work and have a potential chilling effect on university-industry interactions. The full impact of these regulatory changes should be carefully evaluated before they are implemented. . . .

Steps Toward Reform

Protocols should be established to address statutorily mandated regulatory concerns. When new laws are passed by Congress to achieve important public policy goals, unintended regulatory burden can be an unfortunate by-product. When requirements create unintended regulatory burdens for universities, a fast-track approach to amending the law would be a useful tool that could help to minimize burdensome regulations.

Mechanisms should be developed to allow universities to be exempted from certain regulatory and reporting requirements, when appropriate, and if not exempted, to more easily be reimbursed for their associated costs. There are three ways in which this can be done.

First, research universities should be given exemptions similar to those provided to small entities under the Regulatory Flexibility Act (RFA). . . . The RFA encourages tiering of government regulations or the identification of "significant alternatives" designed to make proposed rules less burdensome. The law should be amended to include organizations engaged in conducting federally sponsored research and education activities.

Second, coverage provided under the Unfunded Mandates Reform Act (UMRA) should be extended to research universities. It is often not a single regulation that creates compliance challenges, but the stacking of regulations over time. Agencies rarely reevaluate, eliminate, or redesign regulatory schemes to reduce the burden of compliance. The UMRA requires Congress and agencies to give special consideration to the costs and regulatory impact of new regulations on state and local governments, as well as on tribal entities. Extending coverage to public and private universities would result in research funding agencies being more responsive to the cost burdens of new requirements.

Third, institutions should be allowed to better account for new regulatory costs and to charge these costs to federal awards. . . .

Finally, cost-sharing policies that are appropriate for the research community and that differentiate universities from for-profit entities should be developed. Although a cost-sharing commitment between government agencies and industry partners may be appropriate, requiring the same commitment from university partners ignores universities' educational and public service roles and their nonprofit status. . . .

To better address regulatory issues at research universities, we need new and more timely and flexible mechanisms for universities and associations to work with federal officials. . . . Only by working together can research universities and the federal government reach the shared goal of reducing undue regulatory requirements while maintaining safety and accountability. A more balanced regulatory load would help ease financial burdens on universities and improve the morale and productivity of the researchers whose discoveries and innovations will drive our nation's economy in this century.

> *"Scientists who are granted public support must, through their research, be able to show that the value of their work justifies the infringement of liberty involved in gathering public funds."*

Regulation of Government-Funded Scientific Research Is Justified

Clark Wolf

In the following viewpoint, Clark Wolf argues that while there are strong reasons why scientists should be able to pursue their work without being restricted by regulations, these are not as applicable to publicly funded research as they are to privately funded research. When people are forced through taxation to pay for research of which they may not approve, their liberty is violated, he says; this may be a more important consideration than the violation of scientists' liberty. In his opinion, this justifies the imposition of regulation on scientific research, although regulations must nevertheless be supported by good and sufficient public reasons. Wolf is a professor of philosophy and the director of bioethics at Iowa State University.

As you read, consider the following questions:

1. What, in Wolf's opinion, makes regulation of publicly funded research less difficult to justify than regulation of privately funded research?

2. According to Wolf, why do some people believe that their liberty is violated when the government funds research of which they disapprove?

3. Where there is disagreement about the need for regulation, on which side of the argument does Wolf believe the burden of proof must fall?

[I have] identified three principal considerations that militate strongly in favor of the liberty to pursue scientific research without impediment. It will be useful to state each of these considerations clearly:

1. Presumption in favor of liberty: The liberty to pursue scientific research is simply one aspect of a more general right against interference from others, at least where our behavior does not threaten harm or risk of harm to others.

2. Freedom of conscience and expression: The liberty to pursue scientific research is implicit in broader protections for other intellectual liberties, including freedom of conscience and free expression.

3. Public reasons requirement: Restrictions on research are only appropriate when they can be supported by *public reasons*. If regulations are based only on private reasons (the religious or moral convictions of the legislator, for example) they constitute an unacceptable limitation of liberty.

If accepted, these three considerations constitute powerful reasons to avoid many restrictions and regulations that impede scientific research.

Public Funding and Reasons in Favor of Regulation

The arguments listed above address *direct* regulation of research: regulations that unconditionally restrict research activities, or which ... create a regulatory regime that provides incentives. Where research is publicly funded, the case for liberty is different, since there are liberty interests on both sides of the case. Public research funding is effected through taxation, and those who are taxed to support research have a legitimate interest in the research they pay for. In effect, where research is publicly funded, the case one needs to make in order to justify regulation is lighter than it is in the case of privately funded research. Consider the arguments that might be made by a taxpayer whose money is used to support research she might find questionable.

First, such taxation involves both coercion and limitation of liberty, and thus requires justification under the *presumption in favor of liberty* discussed earlier. While direct restrictive regulation of scientific research would require similar justification, the argument from liberty would seem, in this case, to favor the rights of taxpayers and not the rights of scientists and researchers. In this case, if regulations are necessary to ensure that research funding can answer the challenge from the *presumption for liberty*, this would constitute a good argument in favor of regulation.

A second argument from the principle of freedom of conscience also provides support for the regulation of funded research: In general, our right of freedom of conscience protects our right to believe and to express whatever we wish, and is considered to be violated where one is forced to express a view one does not accept. But people frequently take this value to be compromised when their tax dollars are used to support endeavors they do not support. Thus, during the war in Iraq, many Americans who disapproved of the war regarded it to be a violation of their right of freedom of conscience that their tax dollars were used to fund a war they did not support. In a similar sense, some people regard it as a violation of conscience that their tax money is used to support research that violates their moral principles. Sometimes this was articulated as an *expressive harm*: "By funding the war with my money, the government forces me to *express* support for a war I do not support." While paying one's taxes is not usually considered to be a fundamentally expressive action, it is easy to understand the view of people who object to their tax money being used in this way. We might call this the "Not with my money!" argument.

But a similar argument arises in the case of controversial research: For example, if federal funds are used to support human fetal stem cell research, taxpayers who are opposed to such research might feel that they are being *forced* to express support for activities they regard as deeply immoral. In this sense, the argument from freedom of conscience provides some significant initial support for the view that this research should not receive public funding. Whether this view is convincing *all things considered* will depend on whether an adequate response can be given to this objection.

A third and closely related argument derives more directly from the requirement that coercive public policies require *public reasons* for their justification. The fact that people disagree about controversial research immediately raises the concern that this expense might not be justifiable to *them* in light of "principles and ideals acceptable to them as reasonable and rational."

Notice that these are the same values we cited earlier in defense of scientific liberty. It seems that the same principles and considerations that support the liberty to pursue research may also provide justification for *constraints* on research that is supported by public funds.

More Oversight of Science Research Is Needed

Increasing NSF [National Science Foundation] funding is seen as a magic bullet needed to bolster our economy, preserve our national security, and educate our youth. As such, the agency has enjoyed strong bipartisan support and annually increasing budgets. The president identified basic research funding one of the key pillars of "winning the future" in his annual State of the Union address.

Spending more money alone will not ensure America's success in science. We need to target the money we spend wisely to realize meaningful scientific discoveries and advances. . . .

NSF grants fund wasteful and controversial projects—many of which have limited scientific benefit. An examination of the agency's grant management uncovers deficiencies in oversight and potential criminal uses of taxpayer funds—casting doubt on the agency's ability to effectively manage its grants and fully leverage proposed budget increases. Finally, a broader look at federal science funding shows that the work of NSF is often duplicative of other federal agencies.

The consensus surrounding the importance of NSF is precisely why it is essential to increase and enhance oversight over agency expenditures. Taxpayers should question whether their science dollars are buying the research that NSF promises.

Tom A. Coburn,
"The National Science Foundation:
Under the Microscope," April 2011.

Public Funding, Public Regulation, Public Responsibilities

While the considerations cited in the previous section might be thought to call into question the entire institution of publicly funded scientific research, it would be inappropriate to conclude that we should eliminate such funding in an effort to protect the interests of the public. There is a strong public interest in pursuing scientific and technological progress, and without public funding this interest would be poorly served. It is crucial, however, to recognize that the arguments in favor of regulation impose a burden of justification on those who allocate funds for research and those who receive and use them.

Without doubt, some public funds will be used to support research that *some* people will regard as immoral or morally questionable. If universal consent and approval were necessary, then it would be difficult or impossible to justify the public support of any science at all. Since we *do* have good reasons to provide public support for science, we must conclude that the requirement of universal consent is simply excessive. But this conclusion comes at a cost that must be counted: In this case, the cost is borne by citizens who are compelled, through taxation, to provide funds for research they do not understand and of which they may not approve. I would argue that this justifies reasonable public regulation of funded research, and that it also imposes an important obligation on scientists whose research receives this funding. The obligation in question is not simply an obligation to do good science—it goes without saying that those who receive public support have an obligation to deliver quality. But in addition, there is an obligation to do what one can to ensure that the projects one pursues really do serve the public interest in the end and to do what one can to explain one's research to the public whose tax dollars make it possible. Scientists need to be able to explain the value of their work and to show that it really does merit the use of public resources.

This [viewpoint] began with two pointed questions:

What business do nonscientists have to regulate science?

What legitimate interest (if any) do legislators and the public have to restrict and regulate the professional activities of scientists engaged in research?

When considering regulation in the abstract, it may seem that there are overwhelming reasons to leave scientists alone, as free as possible from regulations that might impede or constrain the process of inquiry. Beyond the minimal restrictions necessary to ensure the integrity of the research process and to protect the rights and interests of those who might be harmed or put at risk by some research, scientists should be free to do as they please.

But where public funds are provided to support research, I have argued that researchers should hold themselves to a higher standard, and the case against regulation is weaker. In effect, the burden imposed by the presumption in favor of liberty falls on scientists, not on regulators. Scientists who are granted public support must, through their research, be able to show that the value of their work justifies the infringement of liberty involved in gathering public funds. Even so, not just any reasons will justify the regulation of scientific practice. We should still avoid regulation that cannot be supported by good and sufficient public reasons.

I have argued that the burden is on *scientists* to defend the value of their research and their claim to public funding. Since public funding relies on taxation, the presumption in favor of liberty imposes the heaviest burden of proof on scientists, not on regulators. Scientists who hope to avoid inappropriate regulations had better be prepared to explain their work, and its value, to those who are compelled to support it.

"The problem of excessive regulatory burdens is itself an issue that puts a drag on the efficiency of all university research."

Regulations That Impede Research Productivity Should Be Reduced

National Research Council

In the following viewpoint, excerpted from a book reporting on problems affecting scientific research in universities, the National Research Council (NRC) discusses changes in government regulatory policies it believes are needed. The NRC recommends that the regulations imposed on universities be reviewed with the goal of eliminating those that are redundant, ineffective, or inappropriate, so that federal research funding can be used more efficiently. The National Research Council is the operating arm of the National Academy of Sciences and the National Academy of Engineering. Its mission is to improve government decision making and public policy, increase public understanding, and promote the acquisition and dissemination of knowledge.

As you read, consider the following questions:

1. What accounts for most of the cost of complying with the regulations imposed on research universities, according to the viewpoint?

2. What order by the Barack Obama administration does the National Research Council believe may lead to a reduction of the regulatory burdens borne by research universities?

3. According to testimony received by the National Research Council, how do primary researchers spend the majority of their time on National Institutes of Health (NIH) grants?

The federal government—OMB [Office of Management and Budget] in conjunction with other federal agencies—should review the regulatory and reporting requirements it imposes on U.S. higher education institutions with the aim of eliminating those that are redundant, ineffective, onerous, or inappropriately applied to the higher education sector. Additions to the reporting or regulatory obligations of universities should be implemented only in light of an OMB cost-benefit analysis and should be accompanied by additional funding to support the higher resulting indirect and administrative costs.

As academic research activities have grown and become more complex, they have become subject to a broad array of regulations. Although state and local governments, as well as universities themselves, promulgate regulations affecting research, federal regulations are the main focus here because they constitute the predominant source of the research-related regulatory burden of universities.

The vast majority of federal regulations are aimed at addressing legitimate issues and risks, and compliance and regulatory oversight are essential to the conduct of federally supported research. AAU [Association of American Universities],

APLU [Association of Public and Land-grant Universities], and COGR [Council on Governmental Relations] affirm that "research universities strongly support the objectives of accountability, transparency, and implementation of important policy and regulatory requirements."

However, the sheer growth of requirements from many federal agencies, a substantial percentage of which were created with other types of organizations (e.g., industry) in mind, has raised the effort and costs necessary for compliance to a significant, unreasonable degree. AAU, APLU, and COGR argue that "in this environment, universities are often forced to institute one agency's compliance requirements across an entire campus, even where they don't make sense, and to sift through each agency's specific rules and develop different compliance mechanisms all aimed at the same ultimate purpose." They continue, noting that the uneven and unsynchronized implementation of regulations and reporting across many federal agencies create "a compliance miasma." . . .

Reviewing federal regulatory and reporting requirements will ensure both that important regulations are effectively enforced and that universities can use federal research funding efficiently and productively. In addition, efforts should be made to shift, where possible, from compliance-driven requirements to incentives for best practices. Most of the cost in compliance (for example, human subjects or animal treatment) is not the actual compliance. Rather, it is in maintaining, checking, and double-checking the bullet-proof audit records required. This is because it is an entirely compliance-driven regime, where the penalties of even a single infraction can be severe. By contrast, in a best-practices regime, an institution would be allowed a (limited) set of trade-offs between the cost of actual compliance and the cost of audit-proof documentation. An example is the system by which ISO-9000 [standards developed by the International Organization for Standardization] certification is awarded. Firms are scored by whether their processes are up to best practices (with a percentage score allowing some variance), not audited at the single-incident level.

The current efforts on the part of the [Barack] Obama administration to address the broad issue of regulatory reform are encouraging. The process put in place by Executive Order 13563, Improving Regulation and Regulatory Review, will hopefully lead to a lowering of regulatory burdens in areas relevant to universities. The ultimate results of this process and impacts on research universities should be evaluated at the appropriate time. A special effort focused on the regulatory burdens on research universities might still ultimately be needed. Fortunately, organizations and institutions that can help facilitate the necessary dialog among research universities and federal sponsors, such as the Federal Demonstration Partnership, are already in existence.

Regulatory Burdens

The problem of excessive regulatory burdens is itself an issue that puts a drag on the efficiency of all university research. The committee received testimony on many specific regulations and issues, several of which will be mentioned here by way of example. The committee endorses this list as a basis for discussions moving forward.

In some cases, experts have identified regulations that do not add value or help ensure accountability, and have proposed alternative approaches. For example, effort reporting is the current mechanism used to support salary, wage, and related charges to federal contracts and grants. Because effort is difficult to measure, the reporting mechanism is of little value as an internal financial control for the institution, while compliance is expensive and the reports are untimely from the standpoint of agency oversight. The current requirement puts a considerable burden on universities, with very little, if any, value to the federal sponsors or to the performing institutions.

The committee therefore recommends that effort reporting be eliminated or significantly modified.

In other areas, such as human subject protection, animal welfare requirements, export controls, management and use of select agents, responsible conduct of research, and financial conflicts of interest, differing implementations and interpretations across agencies can cause inefficiencies in ensuring compliance and raise costs. Standardized approaches to these across agencies would ease compliance burdens on universities significantly.

Further measures aimed at lowering and eliminating regulatory burdens on universities on a continuing basis should be considered. These measures would include the designation of a high-level ombudsman in the OMB's Office of Information and Regulatory Affairs who would be charged with overseeing and regularly reviewing regulations affecting research universities and institutions, perhaps as part of an interagency effort under the National Science and Technology Council. Institutions could apply to the ombudsman to fix or eliminate inefficient regulations that do not add value.

During the course of this study, the committee received substantial testimony concerning the increasingly burdensome administrative and regulatory requirements associated with federally sponsored research imposed upon both institutions and investigators (including the statement that the majority of primary investigator time on NIH [National Institutes of Health] grants is now spent on project administration). Clearly this not only drives up university administrative costs, it also erodes research effort.

> "With increased use of nanoparticles, concerns are growing around the possible harm they may have on humans and other living organisms."

Stronger Regulation of Nanotechnology Research Is Needed for Safety

Adam Soliman

In the following viewpoint, Adam Soliman argues that not enough is known about nanoparticles to be sure they are safe for use in food packaging or in other ways that bring them into contact with food and beverages. Studies have shown that nanoparticles can penetrate the DNA and cells of living organisms, he says, and yet few regulations apply to them. In his opinion, there should be laws requiring manufacturers to research the risks of nano-production and making them accountable for their products. Soliman is the director and founder of the Fisheries Law Centre. He is a researcher focused on legal and economic issues connected with fisheries and seafood.

As you read, consider the following questions:

1. What common use of nanoparticles does Soliman offer as an example of potential for harm?

2. Why, according to Soliman, does the European Union oppose stronger regulation of nanoparticles?

3. According to Soliman, why do existing food safety laws not cover nanotechnology?

Nanotechnology is an innovative science involving the design and application of small-sized particles measuring one hundred nanometers or less. (An average human hair measures 80.000 nanometers in diameter.) Most nanomaterials are derived from conventional chemicals. Their miniscule size and large surface area help to enhance their mechanical, electrical, optical and catalytic features. Thus, nanotechnology is incorporated into a large variety of consumer and health goods, such as food, food packaging, sunblock, chemical fertilizers and animal feed. However, little is currently known about the possible effects of nanotechnology on human, animal or environmental health. What we do know is that nanoparticles have a tremendous ability to penetrate cells and DNA structures. With increased use of nanoparticles, concerns are growing around the possible harm they may have on humans and other living organisms.

Lately there has been a growing international call for stronger legislation on nanotechnology because current laws monitoring its safety and risks are highly insufficient.

Studies show that nanoparticles can easily penetrate DNA and the cells of the lungs, skin and digestive system, thereby causing harm to living organisms. One example of a commonly used but potentially harmful nanoparticle can be found in the beverage industry. Beverage companies have been using plastic bottles made with nanocomposites, which minimize the leakage of carbon dioxide out of the bottle. This increases the shelf life of carbonated beverages without using heavy glass bottles or more expensive aluminum cans. Think of the number of people who are unknowingly being exposed to untested nanocomposites. Nanoparticles are also now being engineered to be more resilient, thereby increasing the risk of causing irreversible damage to living organisms. We simply do not have sufficient data or risk assessment laws in place to analyse whether nanoparticles are safe for consumption.

International Regulations

Legislation governing the use of nanoparticles is limited around the world, particularly in the U.S. In 2007, a report released by the U.S. Food and Drug Administration's [FDA's] Nanotechnology Task Force stated that despite the 'special properties' of nanomaterials, no further regulation is needed.

This report was opposed by environmental group Friends of the Earth and the International Center for Technology Assessment. The organizations filed a petition with FDA urging it to take action to highlight the risks associated with nanotechnology. As a result, the federal [21st Century] Nanotechnology Research and Development Act was passed in 2003.

The Toxic Substances Control Act (TSCA) was also developed to assess the risk posed by substances, and to provide authority to the Environmental Protection Agency (EPA) in regulating them. The TSCA set out provisions to protect living systems against unknown risks of new or engineered substances by regulating and testing new and existing chemicals. However, the EPA does not hold much sway in the American political sphere. In fact, the U.S. legislature does not even require pre-market approval of consumer goods; the FDA relies solely on manufacturers to ensure product safety. Moreover, only evidence of a very specific harm associated with a product can elicit legal restrictions, and nanoparticles have not yet been tested for such specific risks.

The EU [European Union] organization Strategy for Nanotechnology asserts that nanotechnology has the potential to enhance quality of life and industrial competitiveness, and therefore lobbies aggressively for minimal legislation on nanotechnology. Current laws state that anyone producing or importing nanomaterials into Europe is required to provide written notification to public authorities; this notification requires the manufacturer to conduct research illustrating the properties and dangers of the product. However, this research is not monitored, making the data difficult to validate and allowing manufacturers to exaggerate, forge or omit crucial information.

In Hong Kong, the Centre for Food Safety has referred to the World Health Organization's (WHO's) requirement for risk assessment on nanoscale materials for assessing nanoparticles before they can be used in food. Additionally, the Public Health and Municipal Services Ordinance requires all food sold in Hong Kong to be fit for human consumption. But consumer goods lack specific legislation monitoring nanotechnology's expanding applications. Furthermore, no comprehensive and compulsory danger assessment scheme has been introduced to manage the potential risks posed by nanoparticles to public and environmental health.

Demand for Legislation

Internationally, there is a shortage of regulations on nanotechnology due to a lack of accumulated research on the science. As a result, untested nanoparticles seem to slip through the cracks of existing legislation into widely used consumer products. Since the long-term impact of nanomaterials on the natural environment and human health is unknown, it is difficult to comprehensively regulate this technology in a single piece of legislation that would capture its risks. Rather, nanotechnology should be regulated by a series of laws which govern the exposure of nanotechnology on specific areas: food, environment, medicine and agriculture.

Given the increasing use of nanomaterials, comprehensive legislation must soon be developed. Our current juncture offers good opportunities for relevant authorities to make greater efforts in guiding the development of nano-production. Exist-

Federal Policy for Regulation of Nanotechnology

For purposes of regulation and oversight, federal agencies focus on whether the properties or phenomena observed in nanomaterials (and/or their applications) present issues related to risk, safety, benefits, or other regulatory criteria. Federal agencies should avoid making scientifically unfounded generalizations that categorically judge all applications of nanotechnology as intrinsically benign or harmful. In this regard, identification of specific risks in the context in which they arise—based on scientific evidence to support that judgment—will help to ensure that perceptions of specific nanomaterials are based on scientific evidence rather than unsupported generalizations.

Building consumer trust and confidence in a sound regulatory regime is integral to fostering innovation and promoting the responsible development of nanotechnology applications. Federal agencies will strive to provide their stakeholders with clear information that delineates the specific risks identified and the context in which they arise. It is important that federal agencies manage expectations realistically—neither overselling nor underselling the potential benefits or risks.

*"Policy Principles for the U.S. Decision-Making
Concerning Regulations and Oversight of Applications
of Nanotechnology and Nanomaterials,"
Executive Office of the President, June 9, 2011.*

ing laws are scattered across new/toxic substances, public health and food regulations, areas in which action is only demanded once a clear risk is proven. But such proof is not yet available for this technology.

Manufacturers should legally be required to research nano-production and its risks. In addition, a mandatory safety reporting scheme should be introduced to monitor the risks of nanomaterials present in imported and sold products. This reporting scheme should be required for distribution of nanoparticles in any amount to ensure that manufacturers are accountable for all of their products. These safety regulations would hopefully provide protection for consumers until sufficient research can prove that the benefits outweigh the risks of utilizing engineered nanoparticles. Governing bodies can also be responsible for collecting relevant data and establishing a centralized research authority that monitors nanoparticles' long-term effects. This would create awareness and offer the consumer a choice between products that include nanoparticles and the ones that don't.

Nanotechnology is a new science that lacks clear definition and regulations for managing these particles. Untested nanomaterials are already widely engineered into food, medical and agricultural products. The lack of research and management in place for the vast application of nanoparticles makes legislation challenging. Meanwhile, various interest groups lobby strongly for limited legislation on nanotechnology in efforts to allow this science to come to full fruition. The long-term effects of nanoparticle use may be positive, but they may also have a negative impact on health. Thus, jurisdictions should continue to broaden legislation monitoring the development of nanotechnology.

> "What is at stake . . . is nothing less than the question of how to preserve technical innovation in the face of wall-to-wall regulation."

Regulatory Impediments Hinder Innovative Research in Medicine

Richard A. Epstein

In the following viewpoint, Richard A. Epstein discusses the way in which excessive regulation by agencies such as the US Food and Drug Administration (FDA) impedes innovation in medicine and other areas of research. The failure to allow physicians informed by expert organizations to make their own decisions about new drugs not only slows progress but also causes much needless patient suffering, he says. He argues that Congress is not qualified to make decisions about technology, and congressional regulation stifles the people who are qualified. In his opinion, unless the regulatory process is reformed, scientists will move to other countries and the nation will lose its superiority in innovative research. Epstein is a professor at New York University School of Law.

As you read, consider the following questions:

1. What major medical advance, in Epstein's opinion, might not have occurred if the FDA's present regulatory policies had been in place during the 1920s?

2. Why, according to Epstein, do companies that develop medical innovations not challenge the FDA's restrictive policies?

3. What damage does Epstein believe has been done by Supreme Court decisions concerning the commerce clause of the US Constitution?

The invention and discovery of insulin, which went from idea to commercialization in a mere three years, contributed more to human beings and their welfare than every single other advance, taken together, with respect to diabetes in the following ninety years, perhaps by an order of magnitude. Similarly, in technology, the first round of innovation results in huge gains, whereas ten times the amount of effort and money is required for the next advancement, resulting in one-tenth the improvement. The FDA [US Food and Drug Administration] has dampened the innovation cycle, because of its belief that aggressive regulations will protect people from abuse and crackpot medicines. The fate of insulin would have been uncertain if the FDA had oversight of the discovery process back in the early 1920s. The unfortunate result of the FDA's modern incarnation is to cut people off from the very medications and medical devices that might be able to save them. The FDA begins with the view that, unless the applicant can prove to the agency's satisfaction that its product or device is safe, no individual—acting alone or with the aid of a physician—is able to make sound judgments, even on matters so close to his personal welfare.

The clash between the FDA and the right of an individual to make health care decisions came to a head in the well-known case of *Abigail Alliance [for Better Access to Developmental Drugs] v. von Eschenbach*, which raised a sustained challenge to the FDA's power to control the use of drugs by patients. That claim was accepted by the initial panel, by a two-to-one majority. Judge Judith Rogers and Judge Douglas Ginsburg found a constitutional right to use potentially life-saving investigational new drugs that had gone through Phase I trials. The majority rested its holding on the autonomy-based rationale that people are entitled to control their own health care destinies. Judge Thomas Griffith dissented. When the case was heard en banc, Judge Griffith's dissent became the majority opinion, and the alliance's constitutional claim was denied. The right to *refuse* medical treatment does today have constitutional status, but the converse right to *accept* treatment decidedly does not. . . .

Nonetheless, that constitutional determination does not answer the policy challenge to the FDA's hegemony. The challenge asks why the FDA should be allowed to exercise a veto once routine Phase I trials have been completed, even though a huge network of private voluntary organizations—individual physicians and their own expert organizations—have vastly greater access to the reliable information needed to make relevant treatment decisions on a patient-by-patient basis. As a matter of institutional design, the FDA represents a long-term regulatory misadventure whose tardy decisions create bottlenecks for innovation and bring about large amounts of gratuitous suffering. Its grip is so strong that the companies that might protest the agency's actions remain silent, lest they face retaliation from the FDA on other matters that they have pending before the agency. In practice, therefore, the burden of dealing with the FDA falls on patient advocacy groups like Abigail Alliance, which often must lead the challenge against an entrenched FDA, which all too often does not understand state-of-the-art techniques in areas in which it alone has the final say.

Barrier to Research: Too Many Regulations

How much of a barrier to greater progress in medical and health research is too many regulations?

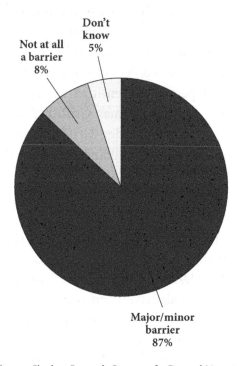

Source: Charlton Research Company for Research!America.

TAKEN FROM: "America Speaks," vol. 4, Research!America, March 2003.

The Need for Reform

What is at stake in this area is nothing less than the question of how to preserve technical innovation in the face of wall-to-wall regulation. The prognosis is grim. Unless we reform agencies like the FDA and their procedures and operations, this country will suffer from a long-term drag on innovation that could, if the trend is not abated, lead to long-term mediocrity, as inventors and scientists flee our shores for friendlier environments. The pace of regulation is one of the central issues of our time. One of the sad consequences of our courts' broad reading of the commerce clause [of the US Constitution] in cases such as *Wickard v. Filburn* [which gave the government the power to restrict farmers' right to grow wheat for their own use] is that it has broadened the scope of federal regulations in a way that has catalyzed these unfortunate results. In dealing with the long-term future of health care, the constitutional disputes over the individual mandate are a sideshow in the search for medical progress. What really matters is ensuring the long-term flow of technology, and that is what regulation is currently stifling.

The question remains how both private and public sources can cooperate in medical and technological advances. Right now, government funding is largely misplaced. Interestingly, the original bioscience grants were quite small. Since the government grants were first introduced, public expenditures have largely shifted from those in basic infrastructure and scientific research to transfer payments, another dangerous trend. That long-term change has thrown yet further obstacles in the path of scientific innovation. The damage done by the New Deal on structural issues continues to manifest itself and even multiply. As a nation, we need to get back on track in the way in which we organize research in the medical, pharmaceutical, biotech, and alternative energy fields. We need to make sure that such research is free of endless regulatory impediments. Vannevar Bush was basically correct in his proposal that the government subsidize research up to the point of proof of principle, but after that, leave inventions to the patent system.

Lastly, we should ask whether the government could, on its own initiative, make intelligent decisions regarding investments in science and technology. The answer: not unless it can find ways to delegate these decisions to people who know what they are doing. The 535 members in the United States

House and Senate do not. Therefore, they cannot be the ideal group to decide whether to subsidize a wind technology that shuts down in calm weather and solar power that does not work at night. No lawyer-dominated institution can answer these questions, but by the same token the scientists and technocrats needed to make intelligent decisions at the center must understand the degree of intellectual freedom needed for science and technology to advance. Finding and supporting those people is difficult in the best of circumstances. But it will prove impossible so long as we operate in a world in which our systems of both subsidies and regulation are misguided. On the one hand, subsidizing new technologies that cannot pay their way in the market is dangerous. On the other hand, risk aversion cannot be the dominant mind-set of regulators. Unfortunately, both these tendencies are deeply ingrained in the regulatory mind-set today. We must change the intellectual climate in order for innovation and growth to regain their footing in the United States.

> *"Because of the inherent risks of adverse impacts, agreement is widespread, even among geoengineering's strongest proponents, that some sort of governance for such tests is needed."*

Scientists Agree That Geoengineering Research Should Be Regulated

David Kramer

In the following viewpoint, David Kramer discusses the controversies expected to arise over research in geoengineering, the deliberate intervention in the earth's climatic system to counteract global warming. There will undoubtedly be extensive debate about whether such technologies should be deployed, but for the time being the most crucial issue is how much experimentation should be done. Without experiments, not enough can be learned in advance of the time when geoengineering may be urgently needed. Although small-scale experiments would have little if any impact on the earth's climate, some scientists fear that public reaction to them might create a backlash that could threaten future research. Kramer is an editor of the science magazine Physics Today.

David Kramer, "Geoengineering Researchers Ponder Ethical and Regulatory Issues," *Physics Today*, December 6, 2013. http://scitation.aip.org. Copyright © 2012 by Physics Today. All rights reserved. Reproduced with permission.

As you read, consider the following questions:

1. According to Kramer, why has the Intergovernmental Panel on Climate Change warned against solar radiation management technologies?

2. Why would existing environmental regulations not prevent an experiment that involved putting large amounts of sulfur into the stratosphere, according to the viewpoint?

3. According to Kramer, what other technology presented ethical problems similar to those that arise with geoengineering, and how were they initially resolved?

As part of a research project exploring stratospheric particle injection to possibly mitigate global warming, a team of UK [United Kingdom] scientists and engineers in 2011 readied an experiment to spray water through a hose tethered to a balloon 1 km [kilometer] above Earth's surface. Although the experiment's environmental impacts would have been nil, leaders of the research ultimately called it off.

In 2012 the indigenous Haida people of British Columbia contracted to dump 100 metric tons of iron sulfate into waters off the west coast of Canada in hopes of stimulating phytoplankton growth and restoring a salmon fishery. Such ocean fertilization also has been proposed for removing and sequestering atmospheric carbon. But the practice is banned by the London protocol on ocean dumping.

As discussion of geoengineering—the deliberate intervention in Earth's climatic system to mitigate global warming—moves from the fringes of science to serious consideration as a possibly last-resort solution, such ethical quandaries are expected to proliferate for experimentalists. The Intergovernmental Panel on Climate Change [IPCC], in its fifth assessment summary for policy makers released on 27 September, mentions geoengineering for the first time. It warns that solar radiation management—the injection of reflective particles into the atmosphere and arguably the most controversial geoengineering approach—could alter the global water cycle and would do nothing to slow ocean acidification.

Although debate has arisen over who decides whether geoengineering technologies will ever be deployed, the more urgent issue for researchers is the sanctioning of outdoor experiments that must occur long before deployment. Because of the inherent risks of adverse impacts, agreement is widespread, even among geoengineering's strongest proponents, that some sort of governance for such tests is needed.

A Slippery Slope

No national or international governance for geoengineering experiments currently exists, and not surprisingly for such a controversial subject, no consensus has emerged on the form it should take. Some organizations, such as the ETC Group, an environmental organization based in Ottawa, Canada, argue for a ban on all outdoor experimentation. But geoengineering researcher David Keith of Harvard University and others advocate a voluntary code of conduct that would only have to be adopted by a handful of funding agencies in the US, Europe, and Asia.

"There are legitimate fears of a slippery slope, and there is a fundamental lack of regulation," Keith said at a September meeting of a National Research Council (NRC) committee that is assessing geoengineering research. "If someone really wanted to put large amounts of sulfur into the stratosphere over the US, it's not obvious what regulations would bind," he warned. The Clean Air Act doesn't apply because, for one thing, it regulates only fixed emissions sources, and the Kyoto Protocol [an international treaty concerning climate change] doesn't apply because sulfur is not on its list of greenhouse gases. Federally funded experiments in the US could require an environmental assessment first, but no such restriction would apply to privately financed experiments. The lack of restrictions will create perceived—and possibly real—problems if large experiments do proceed.

In its 2009 report "Geoengineering the Climate: Science, Governance and Uncertainty," the UK's Royal Society called for international scientific organizations to join in developing a code of practice for research and a voluntary research governance framework. The UK House of Commons Science and Technology Committee and the US House Committee on Science, Space, and Technology cooperated on geoengineering investigations that produced reports in 2009 and 2010. Both endorsed the Oxford principles, a set of five conditions drafted by a team of scholars, under which geoengineering research should be allowed to proceed. Those principles state that research should be regulated in the public interest, public engagement should be sought in the decision making, the research results should be publicly disclosed, the results should be independently assessed, and robust governance structures should be in place before any geoengineering technology is deployed.

Steve Rayner, a political anthropologist at Oxford University and an author of the principles, says the degree and formality of governance should vary with the severity of the potential side effects. "If you were talking about sulfur aerosols in the atmosphere, it would seem that unless you were up for a great deal of international conflict, it's not something you would do without an international agreement," he says. On the other hand, the planting of trees to serve as a carbon sink could be reasonably governed with existing planning and environmental protection laws.

Many Approaches

Keith has proposed that NSF [National Science Foundation] and a few other funding agencies, such as the European Research Council and the Chinese Academy of Sciences, develop a nonbinding memorandum of understanding (MOU) spelling out how they propose to evaluate experiments. Terms might include independent risk assessment, transparency, and degree of usefulness. Only a handful of agencies would need to sign the agreement, Keith said. "An MOU like that would tend to bind the research of even agencies that didn't sign it," he explained to the NRC committee, since other, non-signatory funders would look to the MOU for guidance in reviewing research proposals they may receive.

Other parties argue for a more formal system of governance. Although his organization hasn't backed a particular approach yet, Mark Lawrence, scientific director of the Institute for Advanced Sustainability Studies in Potsdam, Germany, says that an international governance framework should be put in place before any field experimentation is done. "Our deep concern is with the potential for backlash and how that may hinder future basic science," he says.

Scott Barrett, a Columbia University economist, advocates for an international agreement under the auspices of the United Nations (UN). But the regime can't be so heavy-handed that it loses participation from countries that are in a position to do geoengineering, he told the NRC panel. He added a note of realism: "The idea that people are going to spend a lot of effort and go right to high-level laws on things that aren't happening and may not ever happen is kind of naive."

Barrett disagreed with hard-liners who argue that no geoengineering research should be done. "Do you really want to do nothing until we're in a very, very tight situation, and is it really plausible to think that you're going to get 193 countries to do nothing about this through an international agreement?" he asked.

To an extent, the ethical situation facing geoengineering is analogous to the advent of recombinant DNA [rDNA] technology in the mid-1970s. In that case, scientists agreed to an international moratorium on gene-splicing research until a code of conduct on biosafety, now known as the Asilomar principles, was developed. In the US, the National Institutes of Health created a committee of external advisers to review the safety and ethical issues involved with grant proposals involving rDNA. David Winickoff, an ethicist at the University of California, Berkeley, told the NRC panel that a geoengineering advisory committee could review experimental proposals, ensure public disclosure and access to results, perform annual reviews of the science, and reach out to other nations' governance bodies.

Lawrence thinks a likely scenario is for the scientific community to develop a code of conduct that will be administered by an international organization—perhaps the UN Framework Convention on Climate Change or the international Convention on Biological Diversity—or, alternatively, that will be adopted by the funding agencies of the research-funding nations.

Matt Watson, who heads the research project SPICE (stratospheric particle injection for climate engineering), which had planned to spray water from the tethered balloon, disputes news reports that blamed public opposition for cancellation of the experiment. A small element of the overall research project, the experiment was delayed to the point where it became less useful, he says. "From the standpoint of someone who was about to conduct an experiment that had absolutely no climate signature whatsoever, I would argue that a level of preexisting governance would have helped that experiment," he says. "We were going to make sure it was safe and very well communicated and legal. But we thought it might be used by other people to legitimize outdoor research that everybody would be uncomfortable with."

Watson favors strong international governance and says that it must include representation from outside the US and Europe. The governing body he foresees would register experiments, ensure the transparency and communication of the results, and review proposals for scale and possible adverse effects.

Negligible Impacts?

A key point of division in the governance debate is over whether outdoor experiments below a certain size should be allowed to proceed without approval. Keith, a proponent of such a threshold, has proposed an experiment that would deliver 1 kg of sulfur and 100 kg of water by balloon into the stratosphere and observe the effects. He says the experiment could help inform models that predict whether stratospheric sulfate injection could keep Earth's temperature within safe levels. Keith suggests that his experiment is sufficiently small, as measured by its estimated annual impact on radiative forcing, to be allowed to proceed without a specific ethical review.

But others interviewed say there should be no threshold level for experiments. Watson, for instance, agrees that Keith's experiment would be inconsequential climatologically and its effects so small that he would have trouble even detecting them. But, he says, "the social impacts and the reverberations around undertaking that experiment are significant. I don't know if they can or should be predicted or managed." Intentions are very important, he says; if the experiment was labeled as something other than geoengineering, no one would care. He points to a 2011 experiment on cloud microphysics that was performed off the coast of Monterey, California. Although much larger in scale than SPICE and having what Watson says was "a profound effect on the local climate," the experiment created no public stir because few people realized at the time that it was related to geoengineering. "People release atmospheric tracers for experiments all the time, but because it's about atmospheric chemistry and looking at weather systems, nobody would ever object to them."

Lawrence argues that potential backlash from even very small-scale experiments involving solar radiation management could threaten research in noncontroversial areas of atmospheric research as well. He notes how the 2012 ocean fertilization incident off Canada may influence the changes being made to the London protocol that will make it difficult for non-climate-related research on surface water nutrient cycling to proceed. The 87 countries that are parties to the protocol agreed in 2010 to ban ocean fertilization for other than scientific research purposes; they also established a framework for assessing such experiments that does not include a threshold.

> "While most genetic researchers are pushing for more flexibility, the 'ethics establishment' represented by the hard left and ultra-right-wing groups have a vested interest in the status quo."

Tight Regulation of Stem Cell Research Prevents Investment Required for Progress

Jon Entine

In the following viewpoint, Jon Entine discusses the problem of excess regulation that confronts stem cell researchers, which he says is the result of pressure from both the Right and the Left. Researchers have to seek approval from multiple committees before they can begin work, resulting in many projects never even getting started. In Entine's opinion and in the opinions of the experts he quotes, such strict oversight is no longer necessary. For significant medical uses of stem cells to be developed, companies will have to invest in them, which they will not do until research has shown that such uses are feasible. According to Entine, reducing the number of outdated regulatory restrictions can help make this happen. Entine is executive director of the Genetic Literacy Project and a senior fellow at the Center for Health & Risk Communication at George Mason University.

As you read, consider the following questions:

1. According to Entine, what types of activists are responsible for the excessive regulatory restrictions on stem cell research?

2. Why, according to Entine, have many stem cell researchers left the United States for other countries?

3. What major change in the nature of stem cell research has occurred since the oversight established as a result of debates in 2001, according to Entine?

Human genetic technology in general and stem cell research in particular face a challenging future despite the more flexible federal standards introduced by the [Barack] Obama administration. The problems emanate from both the Left and the Right.

Precautionary-obsessed organizations like the Center for Genetics and Society and religious activists such as the Center for Bioethics and Culture—whose views about stem cell research are often at odds—have cowed researchers and cautious health administrators, and emboldened science-wary legislators to set perilously high regulatory barriers for stem cell research.

Consider the situation in California, which is more enlightened on this issue than most other states. Human stem cell researchers need to seek approval for projects from an Institutional Review Board, the Institutional Animal Care and Use Committee and an Embryonic Stem Cell Research Oversight Committee, or ESCRO, before even getting started. Needless to say, the walls of regulation are high enough to scuttle many research projects well before liftoff. That has sent compliance costs soaring and encouraged stem cell researchers to seek haven in less conflicted countries, particularly in Asia.

The paralyzing state of affairs has troubled Hank Greely, the Stanford University bioethicist and lawyer known for his independent streak. Now, in an article in *Nature Medicine*, Greely argues forcefully that the moment for change has finally arrived.

Greely has been refreshingly aggressive in his support for gradually dismantling the ethical and legal hurdles that have limited stem cell research. For example, he strongly endorsed Judge Royce Lamberth's July 2011 38-page decision on behalf of the National Institutes of Health in *Sherley v. Sebelius*, which effectively ruled in favor of relatively unfettered federally funded human embryonic stem cell research by rejecting the claims of "embryo protection" groups.

A Different Era

The current situations—tight restrictions and the proliferation of stand-alone institutional oversight committees—emerged out of the 2001 national debate capped by President George [W.] Bush's controversial decision to restrict but not end federal support of stem cell research. In the wake of the public discussion that ensued, the U.S. National Academies called for the establishment of so-called 'embryonic stem cell research oversight committees' across the country.

It was an understandable policy response then, but times have changed. We've moved from an era of debating ethics about a technology in its infancy to one of advancing science and applied research, Greely argues. "It's not rocket science anymore. A lot of [human embryonic stem cell research] is pretty routine, and it doesn't necessarily need a unique institution to deal with it."

The *Nature Medicine* article follows on the heels of a commentary Greely wrote on what he called "the great ESCRO experiment" in the January issue of the *American Journal of Bio-*

ethics. He suggested that the day-to-day responsibility for research oversight might be moved to existing review boards and committees. Other commentators and organizations, including the California Institute for Regenerative Medicine, challenged his position on grounds that we are not yet ready to step away from such intense ethical scrutiny.

His main contention: Regulations can breed a kind of languor in which restrictions are kept in place out of complacency. That's the surest way to kill innovation. In the case of stem cell research, "It's not saying these guys have been failures and we should get rid of them," he writes. "It's almost saying, 'These guys have been so successful that they worked themselves out of a job'—and that's not a bad thing."

While most genetic researchers are pushing for more flexibility, the "ethics establishment" represented by the hard left and ultra-right-wing groups have a vested interest in the status quo and are resisting.

Greely is hoping to create enough breathing room so private industry can step in and spur research in stem cells beyond the boundaries circumscribed by tight ethical restrictions.

"If stem cells are ever going to make a significant medical contribution . . . there has to be some source of funding for the kinds of basic research that are going on now," he has said. "The field needs to advance to a certain level before companies see the opportunities and are willing to invest their own money in the more development-oriented kinds of research." Chipping away at outdated regulatory restrictions can help make that happen.

| *"At a time when malevolent actors are actively seeking biological weapons of mass destruction, scientists have succeeded in creating an organism that we have all prayed nature would not."*

There Is Inadequate Regulation of Scientific Research Useful to Terrorists

Jim Sensenbrenner

In the following letter sent to White House science advisor Dr. John Holdren, Congressman Jim Sensenbrenner points out that the danger of genetically altered viruses being used by terrorists to create biological weapons is very great. He questions whether scientists ought to do research that creates such threats and suggests that government regulation of such research is inadequate. In Sensenbrenner's opinion, more oversight is needed. Sensenbrenner is a member of the US House of Representatives from Wisconsin and vice chair of the House Committee on Science, Space, and Technology.

As you read, consider the following questions:

1. According to the viewpoint, why did the National Science Advisory Board for Biosecurity recommend that details of research involving the H5N1 avian influenza virus should not be published in scientific journals?

2. Why, in Sensenbrenner's opinion, was the government's response to the H5N1 research inadequate?

3. According to Sensenbrenner, under what conditions would the editor of the journal *Science* be willing to withhold detailed information about scientific research?

Last summer [in 2011], two research teams funded by the National Institutes of Health (NIH) genetically modified the H5N1 avian influenza virus making it capable of respiratory transmission between ferrets, and presumably, between humans as well. The National Science Advisory Board for Biosecurity (NSABB) recommended that journals refrain from publishing the details of the research because it believed that the benefits were outweighed by the risk that terrorist groups could use it as a recipe to create a biological weapon. Yesterday, NIH announced that it will ask the NSABB to reconvene to reexamine new versions of the two studies.

The specter of a deadly flu pandemic is truly frightening. While explaining its recommendation, the NSABB asked, "Could this knowledge, in the hands of malevolent individuals, organizations or governments, allow construction of a genetically altered influenza virus capable of causing a pandemic with mortality exceeding that of the 'Spanish flu' epidemic of 1918?"

The risk of biological attack is great enough that Secretary of State Hillary Clinton took the unusual step of travelling to Geneva to address the United Nations Biological Weapons Convention review on December 7, 2011. Clinton warned that the threat of biological weapons could no longer be ignored and that "there are warning signs," including "evidence in Afghanistan that . . . al-Qaida in the Arabian Peninsula made a call to arms for—and I quote—brothers with degrees in microbiology or chemistry to develop a weapon of mass destruction.'"

The outstanding question is less about why the NSABB is recommending against publication than it is about why this research was performed at all. I place great value on open scientific research and the free flow of ideas—these principles are truly the foundation for innovation and scientific advancement—but in the present case, researchers have created an organism that, if released, could kill millions of people worldwide. At a time when malevolent actors are actively seeking biological weapons of mass destruction, scientists have succeeded in creating an organism that we have all prayed nature would not.

The administration's response has appeared ad hoc, delayed, and inadequate. The NSABB's recommendation against publication came only after the research was finished and submitted for publication. According to Dr. Anthony Fauci, director of the National Institute of Allergy and Infectious Diseases, the health and security risks of the H5N1 research "didn't hit the radar screen" either in the home research institutions or during the NIH's multilayered review system.

Highlighting the danger, Dr. William Schaffner, professor and chair of the Department of Preventive Medicine at Vanderbilt University School of Medicine, argued that it may already be too late to control the research. Dr. Schaffner said, "We already have a growing pyramid of people who know all these data, and that pyramid will continue to grow over time."

The NIH's recent request that the NSABB reconsider its recommendation only adds to the confusion. An ad hoc approach is inadequate to balance the priorities of public health and the free flow of academic ideas. Further, if circumstances pose a legitimate threat to global health, the government needs

A Dual View of the Science

The anthrax attacks that closely followed the 9/11 terrorist attacks [that is, the September 11, 2001, terrorist attacks on the United States] helped create a sense that danger was everywhere. They also helped create a crisis for science. Government statements that the anthrax attacks had most likely been carried out by a U.S.-based microbiologist who had obtained the deadly Ames strain of *Bacillus anthracis* from a culture collection raised serious concerns about the security of potentially dangerous biological agents as well as the trustworthiness of scientists. The U.S. public began to take a dual view of the scientific community: capable of doing both great good (lifesaving medical treatments) and great harm (research that could be abused by terrorists).

Ronald M. Atlas, "Securing Life Sciences Research in an Age of Terrorism," Issues in Science and Technology, Fall 2006.

a review system that is capable of identifying and preventing the spread of dangerous research, ideally before the research is conducted. Broad oversight is needed at both national and worldwide levels by objective scientists with knowledge in the relevant fields.

Questions That Need Answering

Please respond to the following questions by March 31, 2012:

1. How does the NSABB weigh the potential risks and benefits of dual use research? When does it advocate against publication?

2. What systems exist to identify and, if necessary, control early stage dual-use research?

3. *Science* editor Bruce Alberts said that he takes the NS-ABB recommendations seriously and was willing to withhold some information, but only if the government creates a system to provide the missing information to legitimate scientists who need it. What is the government's current system for disseminating legitimate dual-use research worldwide? How is that system being implemented with respect to the articles in question?

4. Is the NIH's review system adequate to identify potentially dangerous dual-use research? Why did it fail to identify the avian flu research until it was completed and submitted for publication?

I appreciate your attention to this matter and look forward to your response.

Periodical and Internet Sources Bibliography

The following articles have been selected to supplement the diverse views presented in this chapter.

David Cyranoski	"US Scientists Chafe at Restrictions on New Stem-Cell Lines," *Nature*, June 4, 2013.
Economist	"The Great Innovation Debate," January 12, 2013.
Yolande Grisé	"Unshackle Government Scientists and Let Them Do Their Jobs," *Globe and Mail* (Canada), January 4, 2013.
Philip Hamburger	"The Censorship You've Never Heard Of," *Commentary*, July–August, 2013.
Alok Jha	"Drugs Legislation Is Hampering Clinical Research, Warns David Nutt," *Guardian* (UK), November 4, 2013.
John D. Kraemer and Lawrence O. Gostin	"The Limits of Government Regulation of Science," *Science*, March 2, 2012.
David Kramer	"Overregulation Is Stifling Research, Science Board Warns," *Physics Today*, May 2014.
Erin O'Donnell	"Governing Geoengineering Research," *Harvard Magazine*, July–August 2013.
David B. Resnik	"Perspectives: Freedom of Speech in Government Science," *Issues in Science and Technology*, November 27, 2013.
Katharine Sanderson	"Putting Nanotechnology Regulation Under the Microscope," *Guardian* (UK), June 25, 2013.
Dan Vergano	"Can Federal Scientists Speak Out Freely?," *USA Today*, June 27, 2013.

CHAPTER 3

Should Animals Be Used in Scientific Research?

Chapter Preface

The Ebola virus is an extremely serious infectious disease that causes fever, muscle pain, nausea, diarrhea, and bleeding from mucous membranes, often resulting in organ damage. About two-thirds of the people who contract it die. Outbreaks of this disease have occurred mainly in Africa, and humans are not its only victims. Ebola has killed roughly a third of the wild gorilla population as well as a great many chimpanzees. Researchers fear that this and other infectious diseases threaten the survival of these species.

Scientists have been working to develop a vaccine for Ebola, although so far they have not succeeded. In May of 2014, however, Dr. Peter Walsh and his colleagues published the results of a study showing that an experimental vaccine that failed to work in humans does produce an immune response to the virus in chimpanzees. This has aroused a fierce debate: Should a vaccine that might save countless wild chimpanzees be tested on captive ones?

Opponents of animal testing deplore all use of animals in scientific research, but their objection to experimentation on chimpanzees is particularly strong because chimps are so similar to humans. Chimpanzees' genetic similarity is why they were initially valued as research subjects; in the past, for the sake of medical science, chimps were routinely subjected to invasive and painful experiments leading to physical and psychological damage. Public opinion turned against this, however, and in 2011 the US Institute of Medicine declared that most current use of chimpanzees for biomedical research is unnecessary. The National Institutes of Health (NIH) thereupon stopped approving grant applications involving chimpanzee research and agreed to review projects already in progress. In 2012 and 2013, it retired most of the chimps owned by the government, sending as many as possible to specially designed sanctuaries where they can live out their lives in comfort.

Although the NIH decision does not apply to privately owned chimpanzees, many pharmaceutical companies have agreed to stop using them in testing. An act prohibiting all research on great apes, other than observation under natural conditions, has been introduced in Congress several times between 2010 and 2014 but has failed to pass on the grounds that immense benefits to humans have been provided by such research in the past and more could be expected in the future. Nevertheless, chimpanzee research is being phased out. The US Fish and Wildlife Service has proposed listing all chimpanzees as endangered, rather than just those in the wild; this would strictly limit the types of research that could be done on them.

Yet, what about development of an Ebola vaccine that might save this endangered species? It could not be done without testing, and opinions about the morality of using captive chimps for this purpose are divided. Many believe it will be ironic if wild chimps are allowed to die when they might be saved. Others feel that chimpanzees have rights and should not be experimented on for any purpose when they cannot consent. In fact, in 2013 animal rights groups filed several lawsuits in New York State arguing that chimps should be classed as persons and given legal rights, not merely protection; the suits were dismissed by the courts, but advocates plan to appeal.

The controversy surrounding research on chimpanzees is only one aspect of a much larger question: Is it right, or necessary, to experiment on animals at all? Existing laws and policies require that lab animals be treated humanely, but there is no escaping the fact that many suffer unavoidable pain. Although animal experimentation has been, and still is, vital to many types of research, extremists in the animal rights movement contend that animals are morally equal to people and that human benefits do not justify any use of them whatsoever.

The authors in this chapter present varying opinions on the feasibility of alternatives to and considerations in using animals for scientific research.

> *"Experimenting with animals before testing on people is a crucial human rights protection required by the famous Nuremberg Code."*

The Grim Good of Animal Research

Wesley J. Smith

In the following viewpoint, Wesley J. Smith argues that research on animals has been indispensable in developing ways to treat human disease. No one likes the idea of experimenting on animals, he says, and efforts are being made to reduce it to a minimum; however, there is no other way to do the necessary research and check the safety of new drugs. Medical treatments have to be tested on living organisms; if not on animals, then on humans, which in Smith's opinion would be an atrocity. Smith is a senior fellow for the Discovery Institute's program on human exceptionalism. He also consults with the Patients Rights Council and the Center for Bioethics and Culture.

As you read, consider the following questions:

1. According to Smith, what deceptive claim do animal rights groups make in their effort to turn people against animal experimentation?

2. What, according to Smith, would be the result if research on animals was prohibited?

3. How did animal research contribute to finding a drug to
treat AIDS, as reported by Smith?

L ast week, scientists in the U.K. announced a "dramatic"
step forward into understanding and treating Alzheimer's.
Researchers infected mice with prion disease and then experimented with methods to ameliorate the effects. They discovered a drug compound that stopped "the disease in its tracks,"
restoring normal behaviors and preventing memory loss. If
the knowledge gained by using mice can be applied to humans, one scientist believes, it will "be judged in history as a
turning point" in the fight against Alzheimer's.

The news reminded me of what we might call the "grim
good" of animal research and the acute threat against it posed
by the animal rights movement. Animal rights advocates such
as People for the Ethical Treatment of Animals [PETA] and
the Abolitionist movement led by law professor Gary Franci-
one oppose all animal experimentation, no matter the human
benefit. Indeed, because they don't consider humans to have
any greater value than animals, activists consider all animal
experiments to be just as evil as intentionally infecting and
studying human beings.

That message doesn't sell well. So, to convince the public
to turn against animal research, activists claim that animal experiments provide no meaningful human benefit. PETA's website puts it this way:

Animal experiments prolong the suffering of people waiting
for effective cures by misleading experimenters and squan-
dering precious money, time, and resources that could have
been spent on human-relevant research.

The frequency of such criticism may be having an impact. A 2013 Gallup poll showed that 39 percent of respondents believe that "medical testing on animals" is "morally wrong," up from 26 percent in 2001.

Claims such as PETA's are half-truths that tell a lie. Yes, animal research takes time. And yes, findings in animals don't always correlate to use in people. And it is probably true that if we experimented directly on people from the beginning, treatments and cures might be discovered more quickly.

But doing so would be a human rights atrocity. In fact, experimenting with animals *before* testing on people is a crucial human rights protection required by the famous Nuremberg Code.

More than that, if animal research were prohibited, scientific advances would be hopelessly stymied. Such a prohibition would stop *basic research*, investigations into how organisms behave or function, which could never be conducted ethically in human beings.

Moreover, a prohibition would also thwart *applied research*, meaning experiments that look for solutions to identified problems such as the Alzheimer's mouse experiments.

Animal testing also provides a crucial safety check that can inform scientists what won't work, so unnecessary human experiments aren't conducted. That was the pattern in the research that helped transform AIDS from a universally fatal disease into a chronic affliction with which patients are enabled to lead longer and healthier lives.

Here's the story as reported in *Science*: Using non-animal methods, researchers designed a "protease inhibitor that looked extremely promising" as a treatment for HIV. Regulations required that it be safety checked in large animals before human trials, in this case, specially bred dogs, to predict how the medicine would react in a living body.

Unexpectedly, the dogs experienced serious liver damage. That was bad for the dogs, but the adverse outcome saved hu-

Basic vs. Applied Animal Research

The definitions of basic (or fundamental) research and applied (or translational) research are not necessarily clear.... The distinctions between basic and applied research is relevant to the use and regulation of animals in research. Biomedical ethics committees and institutional animal care and use committees (IACUCs), for example, must consider the potential benefits of the proposed research for humans and animals. In addition, animal rights groups are often concerned that basic or fundamental research using animals has no immediate application to humans.

In practice, it can be difficult to distinguish to which domain an activity clearly belongs. For example, an experiment that involves the development of a behavioral task in non-human primates to assess functions of the hippocampus would seem to be very basic research. However, there is clear application of the knowledge in terms of diagnostics or interventions with respect to a wide range of clinical diseases and conditions.... What may look like basic research may have very clear applications. Basic research was critical to the development of medical breakthroughs such as coronary bypass surgery and magnetic resonance imaging (MRI), for example. In the United States and the United Kingdom, ... the focus is now "translational research," bringing together basic scientists and clinicians to develop the best and most effective treatments and interventions.

Diana E. Pankevich et al.,
International Animal Research Regulations:
Impact on Neuroscience Research.
Washington, DC: National Academies Press, 2012.

mans from experiencing such a fate. The failure to pass animal testing forced researchers to revise the chemical structure of the medicine, again using non-animal methods.

Further animal testing showed that the liver problem had been solved, opening the door to subsequent human trials. The rest is history. The drug, Crixivan, became generally available in 1996, allowing HIV patients to live longer and healthier lives. That wouldn't have happened without the animal tests.

Nobody relishes animal experimentation. Indeed, for years, the research industry and the government have cooperated with an important animal welfare initiative known as "the Three Rs"—"replacement, reduction, and refinement"—that aims to reduce the number used in research.

But at some point in the research trajectory, human cell lines, computer models, and the like are not sufficient to adequately test safety and efficacy. Eventually, new medical treatments and approaches have to be initially tested in *living organisms*. That means using either animals or humans. The choice is that stark, and for me, an obvious one.

The next time an animal rights group claims that animal research provides no human benefit, stop and think about the astonishing medical advances made over the last fifty years. Because scientists experimented with research animals, vaccines were developed, new lifesaving medical and surgical techniques were perfected, diseases were cured, extending our lives and alleviating incalculable amounts of human suffering.

"*Animal advocates, as well as many scientists, are increasingly questioning the scientific validity and reliability of animal experimentation.*"

Results from Research on Animals Are Not Valid When Applied to Humans

American Anti-Vivisection Society

In the following viewpoint, the American Anti-Vivisection Society (AAVS) declares that experimentation on animals is not a valid means of testing treatments for human disease. The AAVS maintains that animal studies do not reliably predict human outcomes, that most drugs that appear promising in animal studies go on to fail in human clinical trials, and that reliance on animal experimentation can delay discovery. In the opinion of the AAVS, animals are used in medical research more from tradition than from evidence of scientific value. The AAVS is a nonprofit animal advocacy organization dedicated to ending experimentation on animals in research, testing, and education.

As you read, consider the following questions:

1. According to the AAVS, why is it not valid to apply the results from animals to humans?

2. Why, according to the AAVS, does animal experimentation delay new medical discoveries?

3. In the opinion of the AAVS, for what reasons do some scientists perform too many similar experiments?

Scientists use animals in biological and medical research more as a matter of tradition, not because animal research has proved particularly successful or better than other modes of experimentation. In fact, animal 'models' have never been validated, and the claim that animals are necessary for biomedical research is unsupported by the scientific literature. Instead, there is growing awareness of the limitations of animal research and its inability to make reliable predictions about human health.

The biomedical research community and its affiliated trade associations routinely attempt to convince the general public, media, and government representatives that the current controversy over the use of animals is a life-and-death contest pitting defenders of human health and scientific advancement against hordes of anti-science, anti-human, emotional, irrational activists. Such a deliberate, simplistic dichotomy is not only false, but ignores the very real and well-documented ethical and scientific problems associated with the use of animal experiments that characterize modern biomedical research, testing, and its associated industries.

The biomedical community would instead be better served by promoting increased funding and research efforts for the development of non-animal models that overcome the pressing ethical and scientific limitations of an increasingly archaic system of animal experimentation.

Ethical Concerns of Using Animals in Research

Animals are living, sentient beings, and animal experimentation by its very nature takes a considerable toll on animal life.

In most cases, researchers attempt to minimize the pain and distress experienced by animals in laboratories, but suffering is nonetheless inherent as animals are held in sterile, isolated cages, forced to suffer disease and injury, or euthanised at the end of the study.

While the majority of scientists are well-intentioned, focused on finding cures for what ails us, some biomedical researchers fail to recognize or appreciate that laboratory animals are not simply machines or little boxes that produce varieties of data. Once consideration of animals is reduced to this level, callousness and insensitivity to the animals' pain, suffering, and basic needs can follow.

Indeed, animals in laboratories are frequently treated as objects that can be manipulated at will, with little value for their lives beyond the cost of purchase. AAVS [American Anti-Vivisection Society], however, believes that animals have the right *not* to be exploited for science, and we should not have to choose between helping humans and harming animals.

Scientific Limitations of Using Animals

In addition to the ethical arguments against using animals in research, animal advocates, as well as many scientists, are increasingly questioning the scientific validity and reliability of animal experimentation. Some of the main limitations of animal research are discussed in detail below:

- Animal studies do not reliably predict human outcomes.

- Nine out of ten drugs that appear promising in animal studies go on to fail in human clinical trials.

- Reliance on animal experimentation can impede and delay discovery.

- Animal studies are flawed by design.

Animal studies do not reliably predict human outcomes. Obvious and subtle differences between humans and animals in terms of our physiology, anatomy, and metabolism make it difficult to apply data derived from animal studies to human conditions. Acetaminophen, for example, is poisonous to cats but is a therapeutic in humans; penicillin is toxic in guinea pigs but has been an invaluable tool in human medicine; morphine causes hyper-excitement in cats but has a calming effect in human patients; and oral contraceptives prolong blood-clotting times in dogs but increase a human's risk of developing blood clots. Many more such examples exist. Even within the same species, similar disparities can be found among different sexes, breeds, age and weight ranges, and ethnic backgrounds.

Furthermore, animal 'models' are seldom subject to the same causes, symptoms, or biological mechanisms as their purported human analogues. Indeed, many health problems currently afflicting humans, such as psychopathology, cancer, drug addiction, Alzheimer's, and AIDS, are species specific.

As a result, accurately translating information from animal studies to human patients can be an exercise in speculation. According to [D.G.] Hackam and [D.A.] Redelmeier (2006), "patients and physicians should remain cautious about extrapolating the findings of prominent animal research to the care of human disease," and even high-quality animal studies will replicate poorly in human clinical research.

Nine out of ten drugs that appear promising in animal studies go on to fail in human clinical trials. Indeed, because of the inherent differences between animals and humans, drugs and procedures that work in animals often end up failing in humans. According to Health and Human Services Secretary Mike Leavitt, "nine out of ten experimental drugs fail in clinical studies because we cannot accurately predict how they will behave in people based on laboratory and animal studies."

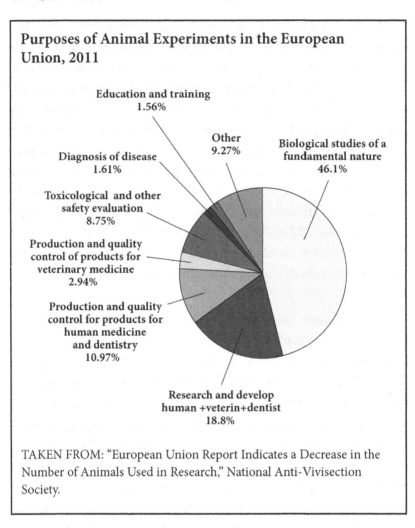

Purposes of Animal Experiments in the European Union, 2011

Education and training
1.56%

Other
9.27%

Biological studies of a fundamental nature
46.1%

Diagnosis of disease
1.61%

Toxicological and other safety evaluation
8.75%

Production and quality control of products for veterinary medicine
2.94%

Production and quality control for products for human medicine and dentistry
10.97%

Research and develop human +veterin+dentist
18.8%

TAKEN FROM: "European Union Report Indicates a Decrease in the Number of Animals Used in Research," National Anti-Vivisection Society.

A significant amount of time and money, not to mention animal lives, is squandered in the process. Pfizer, for example, reported in 2004 that it had wasted more than $2 billion over the past decade on drugs that "failed in advanced human testing or, in a few instances, were forced off the market, because of liver toxicity problems."

In fact, there have been numerous reports recently of approved drugs causing serious and unexpected health problems, leading the Food and Drug Administration (FDA) to remove the products from the market or require black-box warnings on their labels. The FDA has reported that "adverse events associated with drugs are the single leading contributor to preventable patient injury, and may cost the lives of up to 100,000 Americans, account for more than 3 million hospital admissions, and increase the nation's hospitalization bill by up to $17 billion each year." The agency estimates that drug-related injuries outside the hospital add $76.6 billion to health care costs.

Waste of Time and Money

Reliance on animal experimentation can impede and delay discovery. Alternatively, drugs and procedures that could be effective in humans may never be developed because they fail in animal studies. It is difficult to know how frequently this occurs, since drugs that fail in animals are rarely tested in humans. However, there have been some notable cases. Lipitor, for example, Pfizer's blockbuster drug for reducing cholesterol, did not seem promising in early animal experiments. A research scientist, however, requested that the drug be tested in a small group of healthy human volunteers, and it was only then that its effectiveness was demonstrated.

In many instances, medical discoveries are delayed as researchers vainly waste time, money, effort, and animal lives trying to create an animal model of a human disease. A classic example is the discovery that smoking significantly increases the risk of lung cancer. The finding was first reported in 1954 on the basis of an epidemiological study. The report was dismissed, however, because lung cancer due to inhalation of cigarette smoke could not be induced in animal models, and it wasn't until 30 years later that the U.S. surgeon general finally issued the warning on cigarettes.

Another noteworthy example concerns the development of the polio vaccine. Researchers spent decades infecting nonhuman primates with the disease and conducting other animal experiments, but failed to produce a vaccine. The key event which led directly to the vaccine and a Nobel Prize occurred when researchers grew the virus in human cell cultures *in vitro*.

Animal studies are flawed by design. In addition to the fact that animals make poor surrogates for humans, the design of animal experiments is often inherently flawed, making it that much more unlikely that results obtained from such studies will be useful. Researchers from the Vanderbilt University Medical Center described some of the problems with animal 'models' in their 2004 article: ". . . [T]he design of animal studies automatically controls many variables that can confound human studies"; ". . . [T]he phenotypes studied in animals are not truly identical to human disease but are limited representations of them"; and "In most cases, animal studies do not assess the role of naturally occurring variation and its effects on phenotypes."

Furthermore, in their effort to secure research funds, expand the territorial boundaries and influence of their laboratories, or simply maintain their employment, it is a common practice for biomedical researchers to generate an endless series of experiments by devising minor variations on a common theme, redefining previous work, subdividing one problem into multiple parts, or manipulating new technology and equipment to answer old or irrelevant questions. Such practices are endemic in such fields as experimental psychology, substance abuse/addiction, and most of the neuroscience and transplantation protocols, yet by their very design do little to improve human or animal lives.

Promise of Alternatives

In animal research, as with slot machines, if you pull the traditional levers enough times, a winner eventually appears. However, animal research, in addition to being ethically challenged, is also highly flawed and severely limited, and as such, the majority of such research has failed to translate into improvements in human health.

Despite the problems with animal research, there continues to be an overreliance on questionable animal 'models,' and there has been "an unprecedented increase in funding for biomedical research" over the years, without much success.

> "While I (and I believe every scientist) would prefer to unlock the secrets of biomedicine and design treatments to diseases without the use of animals, the technology that would allow that . . . remains science fiction."

Scientific Research on Animals Is Vital to Advance in Medicine

Ross R. Keller

In the following viewpoint, Ross R. Keller explains why he believes it is necessary to use animals in medical research. He points out that almost all medical advances for the past century have involved animal research and that only through this means can scientists discover how disease processes work. Although some people believe animal research is unethical and most scientists would prefer not to do it, in his opinion there is no alternative. Great care is taken, he says, to treat research animals humanely. Keller is a doctoral candidate in biomedical sciences at Penn State College of Medicine.

As you read, consider the following questions:

1. According to Keller, what are the broad categories of research in medicine in which animals are used?

2. Why, according to Keller, is it not possible to learn enough about biological processes by using cell cultures instead of live animals?

3. What are the "three Rs" pertaining to animal research, as explained by Keller?

A question was submitted to our blog asking: "How does animal research advance medicine?" It is an important question, and I will do my best to answer it.

The average human life expectancy has increased dramatically over the past 100 years. In 1900, most did not live past 50. Now, most will live to see their 75th birthday. This increase is largely due to advances in medicine that would not have been possible without animal research.

In fact, many scientific organizations as well as the World Health Organization and the United States Department of Health and Human Services estimate that animal research has played a part in almost every major medical advancement over the past century. This fact alone underscores the importance that animal research has played in medicine.

Despite all the benefits of animal research in advancing medicine, many opponents of animal research ask the question, "What gives humans the right to use another creature for our own advancement?" It's true that this is not a question with an easy answer. Every person has his or her own values and is entitled to his or her own opinion on that question.

In general, animal research falls into two broad categories as it relates to advancing medicine: 1. determining how a disease works, and 2. finding out if a potential treatment is effective and safe.

Replacement, Reduction, Refinement

The concept of alternatives is relatively simple and was first enunciated in 1959 by two British scientists who argued that animal researchers should always follow the principle of the "Three Rs"—Replacement, Reduction and Refinement.

Replacement refers to situations where non-animal techniques may be substituted for techniques using research animals. There are a number of examples of such replacement in the diagnosis of disease and in the testing and standardization of biological therapeutic agents. Rabbits are no longer used in pregnancy tests. Using mice to test the potency of batches of yellow fever vaccine was long ago replaced by a cell culture test....

Reduction refers to cases where the number of animals required for a particular activity or project can be reduced. One example of recent progress comes from the field of acute toxicity testing. Most toxicologists now agree that it is not necessary to use from 60 to 200 rodents to generate the statistically precise lethal dose. One can obtain perfectly adequate lethal-dose data using no more than 10 to 20 animals....

Refinement is a very neglected aspect of the alternatives concept. It refers to the modification of a technique to reduce the pain and distress experienced by research animals. For example, various jacket and tether systems have been developed to protect catheters inserted into research animals which then allow an investigator to administer doses of test chemicals and take blood samples from an animal without having to restrain it.

Andrew Rowan, "The Alternatives Concept," Animal Welfare Information Center Newsletter, *April–June 1991.*

Biological Processes Must Be
Studied in Living Hosts

To answer the basic questions about how a disease or biological process works, one needs to be able to see how all the different cells and organs in the body work together and where something goes wrong. This is not possible with simpler models such as a single cell culture because there are no tissues, organs, or varying cell types.

For example, a tumor that grows in the body cannot be studied as it would be found naturally without a living host. A tumor is a complex tissue that involves cancer cells, immune cells, and several types of support cells as well as a blood supply. Trying to study how a tumor arises or maintains itself using culture methods without eventually verifying those studies in an animal could lead to results that not only do not advance medicine, but in some cases could set it back.

After elucidating how a disease process works, sometimes a vulnerability can be found that could ameliorate or even cure that disease. This vulnerability can sometimes be exploited in the form of a drug. But first, the drug must go through several stages of testing. They begin in cell cultures, and it is determined if the drug functions as it theoretically should—targeting the right molecules within a cell.

However, this is not the end of the process. Oftentimes, a drug may have side effects that are not apparent until the drug is tried on an actual organism. It may not target the same cell when it begins circulating in the body. Or, different dosages may cause different side effects. These questions and more need to be answered before any human treatment can be tried.

Despite the benefits and necessity of animal research, the topic remains a sensitive issue—inciting emotional and forceful opinions on both sides. As a scientist, I must advocate for the use of animals in biomedical research. While I (and I believe every scientist) would prefer to unlock the secrets of biomedicine and design treatments to diseases without the use of animals, the technology that would allow that, at this point in time, remains science fiction.

Research Animals Are Treated Humanely

Society has taken great care to ensure animals used in research are treated humanely.

Any study that requests to use animals must go through a rigorous review via an institutional animal care and use committee (IACUC). Each institution has its own committee, which includes a variety of people including a lay person not involved in research. The committee ensures that the study is run properly and follows federal regulations laid out in the Animal Welfare Act and the Public Health Service Policy on Humane Care and Use of Laboratory Animals.

Furthermore, every medical laboratory in which animals are used for biomedical research takes great care to follow the 3 "Rs." 1. *Reduce* the number of animals used in studies to the minimum necessary. 2. *Replace* animals with other models whenever possible. 3. *Refine* procedures to make sure animals are treated as comfortably and humanely as possible.

Overall, animal research has and will continue to advance medicine in ways most people never even consider. In one way or another, either ourselves or through family members, we have all felt the benefits of animal research—every person who is cured of cancer, every person who lives a long life despite an HIV diagnosis, every person who keeps control of their diabetes, every person who has had surgery with the use of anesthetics (nearly all), every person who takes aspirin for headaches, every person who takes antibiotics for an infection.

The list goes on, and will continue to grow.

> "Imagine how much real good the funds that . . . researchers have used causing monkeys anxiety for 30 years could have done directly serving those children who suffer so greatly."

Not All Scientific Research on Animals Is Ethically Justified

Lori Gruen

In the following viewpoint, Lori Gruen discusses an experiment with monkeys that she believes is not ethical. In this experiment, she says, young monkeys that have been deprived of maternal care will be exposed to frightening stimuli and then killed so that their brains can be studied. In her opinion, it is not clear that this experiment will do anything to alleviate human suffering: first, because monkey brains are not sufficiently comparable to human brains and second, because even if it provided valid information, it would not be the only way to help children who suffer from anxiety. Gruen is a professor of philosophy, feminist studies, and environmental studies at Wesleyan University. She is the author of Ethics and Animals: An Introduction.

As you read, consider the following questions:

1. Why does Gruen believe the experiment with monkeys she is describing violates the spirit of the Animal Welfare Act?

2. Why, according to Gruen, will the examination of the monkeys' brains not provide valid information about the development of neuropsychiatric disease in humans?

3. What does Gruen feel would help children suffering from anxiety more than whatever might be learned from experimenting on animals?

Last month [September 2012] I gave a talk at the University of Wisconsin [UW] at the invitation of the Forum on Animal Research Ethics. This forum has hosted a variety of speakers who discussed different aspects of animal research. I spoke about animal research and the limits of medicine.

I focused on the ways that ethical questions are inseparable from scientific questions. Values are implicated in what we do, particularly when suffering is involved (and I talked about both human and nonhuman suffering). Importantly, just because something is scientifically justified doesn't mean it is ethically justified. If an NIH [National Institutes of Health] panel decides to fund an experiment that doesn't necessarily mean it is an ethically justified experiment. In general, NIH panels tend to defer to the judgments of IACUCs (institutional animal care and use committees) on ethical questions.

But if an IACUC approves an experimental protocol, does that mean it is ethically justified?

Some at UW think so. However, there is one experimental protocol that I learned on my visit was recently approved by not one, but two IACUCs, that I think is not ethically defensible. The protocol is now part of the public record and I have had the chance to carefully review it.

The research in question is a new type of maternal deprivation research designed to study anxiety by creating adverse early rearing conditions and then exposing the maternally deprived young monkeys to a snake and other frightening stimuli. The monkeys will be killed after the experiment is over and their brains will be studied. I believe this experiment is unethical and I also think it violates the spirit, if not the promulgated regulations, of the Animal Welfare Act, which explicitly requires that the psychological well-being of primates be promoted (not intentionally destroyed).

There is no doubt that people who suffer from anxiety disorders suffer considerably and finding a way to alleviate this suffering is a noble end. However, it isn't at all clear that the proposed monkey model will help alleviate human suffering, in part because it isn't clear that the monkey model is adequate.

Brains Develop Differently

Consider the results of a recent study that found distinct differences in myelin development in humans compared to our closest genetic and evolutionary relative, the chimpanzee. Myelin allows the developing brain to build connections that are necessary for cognitive function, including the regulation of emotions. Myelin development happens early in chimpanzee brain development and later in humans, and it is at this time, according to researchers, that humans are vulnerable to neuropsychiatric disease. If the brains of our closest primate relatives are so different than our own, macaque monkey brains will be more profoundly different.

In addition, this approved maternal deprivation experiment, by the researcher's own admission, does not replicate the adverse conditions that children face. As Dr. Sujatha Ramakrishna, M.D., a pediatric psychiatrist, told me, she "sees many patients in our offices who have grown up under 'adverse' conditions, and they are hardly a uniform set. There

BIZARRO—© 2003 Dan Piraro, distributed by King Features.

are a wide variety of stressors that traumatized human children have to deal with, including various types of abuse and neglect, and these can never be replicated with any kind of accuracy using animal models."

Even if there were a promising benefit to be found, there is a second question that needs to be answered in order to determine whether these experiments are ethically justified—is there no other way to achieve the benefit? In the case of this maternal deprivation experiment, there are many obvious ways to minimize the human suffering that results from anxiety disorders. If children are suffering from early adverse rearing conditions, social programs that work to prevent this adversity, for example, programs that teach young mothers parenting skills; programs that help fight drug addiction; programs that provide affordable access to prenatal and early childhood health care; affordable child care programs that can also monitor adverse exposures; as well as adult services for parents to address alcoholism, anger management, and provide job training, could all directly help. Having such services more readily available can prevent the psychological harms that arise from childhood trauma and would have other social benefits as well. In tough economic times, the provision of such services generally fall on charities that are already overburdened.

When federal taxpayer dollars go to fund animal experimentation, these funds cannot be used in other ways. Imagine how much real good the funds that UW researchers have used causing monkeys anxiety for 30 years could have done directly serving those children who suffer so greatly and have very limited access to care and assistance. Researchers claim there is a moral imperative to conduct primate research to help prevent human suffering. I agree there is a moral imperative here to help children who are suffering. But research that involves creating monkeys' [anxiety] and intentionally damaging their psychological well-being will not help these children, and it will use valuable resources that actually could go a long way toward helping people who suffer from anxiety live better lives.

> "Animal research plays an integral role in scientific study relevant not only to furthering our basic understanding and knowledge but also to informing clinical practice and public health policy."

Opposition to Animal · Studies Threatens Research in Psychology

Allyson J. Bennett

In the following viewpoint, Allyson J. Bennett discusses the value of animal research, especially in the field of psychology, and the campaigns that currently threaten it. The public does not understand animal research, she says, and its opponents are making headway in their effort to end it, as membership in animal rights groups is increasing. In her opinion, if animal rights activists succeed in eliminating research on animals, there will be serious consequences not only for scientific research but also for human health. She says that progress in understanding factors that contribute to disease will no longer be possible. Bennett is a researcher in psychology and a faculty member at the University of Wisconsin-Madison.

As you read, consider the following questions:

1. What extremist tactics are being used by radical animal rights groups, as reported by Bennett?

2. What, in Bennett's opinion, are the wider implications of recent decisions to reduce the amount of research done on chimpanzees?

3. According to Bennett, why are some scientists unwilling to speak out publicly in defense of animal research?

Research with nonhuman animals occupies a central and essential role in psychology and related fields. Both old and new discoveries from animal research continue to play key roles in advancing our understanding of human behavior. Studies in a wide range of nonhuman animals were foundational—and remain critical—to identifying how specific brain areas or neurotransmitters contribute to healthy development and function. Studies of language, communication, cognition, and emotion in great apes fundamentally changed how we think about development, our own abilities, and evolution. They also informed how we should best care for other primates and underscored the importance of conservation. Understanding of genetics, epigenetics, immunology, pharmacology, physiology, development, and a full range of other topics depend on a science that includes animal studies. Animal research plays an integral role in scientific study relevant not only to furthering our basic understanding and knowledge but also to informing clinical practice and public health policy. It is for this reason that psychologists need to become informed about the threats to research conducted with nonhuman animals.

The use of animals in research is often misunderstood. Much of the public is not familiar with the ethical guidelines and strict federal, state, and local regulations that govern the care and use of animals in research. Almost all scientists approach research with compassion and a commitment to responsible, humane, and ethical treatment of animals, and it is often their discoveries that lead to improvements in animal welfare and health. It is also true that the ethical principles that govern animal research include the replacement of animal models, and use of less complex species, when possible. Among other reasons, this has led to the decreased need for and use of great apes such as chimpanzees in various types of biomedical research.

Anti-Animal Research Campaigns

Chimpanzee research achieved new levels of attention within both the public and scientific sphere in the last year. Attention to its current status and future are reflected in broad and sustained news coverage, intense debate, and emotional pleas delivered via mainstream and social media by scientists, scientific societies, animal protection groups, and animal rights activists. . . .

Public discussion about animal research is not new. Ending all use of animals in research has always been a goal of a number of passionate, organized, sometimes militant, and sometimes terrorist, animal rights groups. Perhaps most visible among them is the People for the Ethical Treatment of Animals (PETA). The group, whose leader famously equated rats and children, saying "A rat is a pig is a dog is a boy," recently celebrated its 30th anniversary. It also recently launched its third demographically targeted website, PETA Prime. Entire generations have grown up with exposure to PETA through publications placed in school libraries; multiple dynamic, widespread face-to-face outreach; and the publicity stunts for which the group has gained broad public name recognition.

Animal rights groups have increased their membership and reach over the past several decades. The largest, the Humane Society of the United States (HSUS), claims 11 million members ("1 in every 28" of Americans) and has assets of more than $187 million dollars. Others, including the Animal Liberation Front and Negotiation Is Over, have continued to develop, advocate and execute tactics that borrow a page from other extremist groups and seek to intimidate scientists. Increasingly, they are focusing harassment, threats, and fear campaigns on individual researchers and lab staff rather than at the institutions that support their research.

A Multipronged Approach to Eliminating Animal Research

These groups differ in their tactics, scope, and in some aspects of their philosophies and agendas. Nonetheless, they are united in their understanding of the importance of public opinion in their long-term success. They understand that if the majority of the public can be convinced—no matter how false such a conclusion may be—that animal research is not valuable, not necessary, and not morally correct, the work will not be supported and will ultimately end. In fact, the leadership of HSUS has declared that a complete elimination of *all* animal research is an achievable goal by 2050.

Animal rights groups have invested considerable energy, significant resources, and sustained commitment to advancing an agenda to serve their goal of eliminating all animal research. The recent events surrounding chimpanzee research reflect just a small portion of this agenda. . . . An Institute of Medicine [IOM] panel was commissioned by the National Institutes of Health to consider whether biomedical and behavioral research with chimpanzees is necessary. The panel's report, which recommended limiting the use of chimpanzees in research, was released in December 2011. Its recommendations were immediately accepted by Dr. Francis Collins, the director of the National Institutes of Health. Dr. Collins announced a moratorium on new funding for chimpanzee research pending the development of implementation guidelines. Speaking of research, an animal research education and advocacy group (of which I am a member), has posted a number of articles on this issue. In one we summarize the IOM report as follows:

> The report acknowledged that chimpanzees were vital to past progress, but that at present there is limited necessity and justification for them in research. It did not endorse a ban on chimpanzee research, nor the continuation of the moratorium on breeding, stating that these could potentially cause "*unacceptable losses to the public's health.*" It also made clear that "*animal research remains a critical tool in protecting and advancing the public's health*".

The IOM report and NIH announcement are significant events in the history of animal research in the U.S. They hold many implications for the future of our field. The report, GAPCSA [Great Ape Protection and Cost Savings Act], and media coverage are focused on chimpanzees. It is clear, however, that the real issue they signal applies to all animal research and deserves more serious consideration by members of the larger scientific community, whether or not they engage in animal research. There should be no doubt that groups working to end all animal studies view chimpanzee research as only the first and easiest target. It is not clear, however, that the members of academic and scientific communities—most of whom recognize that humanely conducted animal studies are essential to both basic and biomedical research—perceive that the recent events may serve as a step toward the elimination of a large and important component of the scientific enterprise.

Speaking Up for Animal Research

Over the past 30 years the animal rights community has moved from the margins and into the mainstream. A recent report by the Pew Research Center for the People and the Press, in collaboration with the American Association for the Advancement of Science (AAAS), showed that only 52% of the public support animal research. *Science* magazine recently carried a full-page ad from the animal rights group HSUS urging the scientific community to endorse its call for the end of great ape research. Animal rights groups have pursued outreach and education campaigns aimed at drawing public attention to their point of view. They have used a range of tactics, including the familiar publicity stunts and misinformation campaigns. In this, they often benefit from the fact that much about animal research is not well understood by the public. Exacerbating the problem is that too few voices are raised to present accurate information about the unique importance of animal research to both basic and biomedical science.

Some of the most effective voices would be those of scientists engaged in animal research. But many—though certainly not all—are inhibited by the fear that public engagement can draw fire from activists who focus threats and harassment on scientists who work with animals.

There are other voices that can make a difference in public understanding of the value of animal research. Among them are those members of the academic and scientific communities whose work and goals build on and benefit from the scientific contributions of animal research. Psychologists are among those who are well positioned to assist in this public effort.

Research with nonhuman animals occupies a central and essential role in psychology. Historical and current examples are abundant in our textbooks and our literature. . . .

Making the connections among animal studies, scientific progress, and advances in human health is the critical foundation for public understanding of why animal research is valuable. If people do not understand those connections, or do not understand why we cannot always turn to non-animal alternatives, then they may not appreciate why animal research should continue. Lack of public understanding of science on other fronts—e.g., climate change, vaccines, and evolution—only increases the difficulty of scientists' efforts to convey the importance of animal research.

All of this matters deeply to the future of research, psychology, and human health. A choice to turn away from all animal research will have consequences. We would lose essential avenues for discovery. We would fail to realize continued progress in understanding the neural, behavioral, cognitive, developmental, physiological, genetic and biological processes that contribute to human and animal health and disease. Of special relevance to psychology, we would no longer be able to use the best systems to develop and assess new strategies for prevention and treatment of mental health disorders. Assessment of the safety and efficacy of new medications would be compromised. The remaining path available to us, experimentation in humans, is one rejected many years ago in recognition of its failure on ethical grounds. In the absence of research with rodents (95% of all animal research subjects) and other animal models in which new medications and treatments can be developed and evaluated, new treatments will either not be used or will necessarily involve risky experimentation on humans.

New discoveries in a broad range of fields—gene therapy, epigenetics, neural prosthetics, pharmacotherapy, regenerative medicine—highlight the avenues by which animal studies contribute to our understanding and ability to improve human and animal health. It may be that the public ultimately decides that the benefits are not worth the cost of using animals in research. Our responsibility as scientists is to make sure that the decision is based on accurate information and thoughtful consideration of the full range of issues involved in this complex topic. Scientists engaged in animal research certainly cannot accomplish this alone. They are, however, among those who see the potential implications of the recent IOM and NIH actions concerning chimpanzee research. These actions are not a single, limited case of restricting animal research for which there is nearly universal agreement; rather they may be another step along a trajectory that leads to the end of all animal research.

Responding to the challenges to animal research will require many voices in a sustained effort to advance public education and civil dialogue. These challenges are urgent and require us to dedicate our time and energy now in order to prevent harm to the public in the future.

> "Unlike human-research protections, which are now guided by a principled approach, laws governing the use of animals in research have resulted from a largely politicized, patchwork process."

Replacements Must Be Found for Animals in Scientific Research

Hope Ferdowsian

In the following viewpoint, Hope Ferdowsian discusses the issues raised at a conference on animal research and alternatives to using animals. Regulations for the treatment of research animals are inconsistent, she says, and some species such as mice are not covered by regulations, leaving them subjected to painful experiments. She explains that animal suffering is more severe than has been appreciated in the past and that, in addition to physical pain, laboratory animals experience emotional distress such as depression. Some researchers are discovering alternatives to the use of animals in research, and in Ferdowsian's opinion future generations will wonder why using alternatives to animals did not happen sooner. Ferdowsian is a physician and director of research policy at the Physicians Committee for Responsible Medicine.

As you read, consider the following questions:

1. According to the viewpoint, what was the original purpose of the Animal Welfare Act?

2. What animals besides mice are not covered by the Animal Welfare Act, according to Ferdowsian?

3. What, according to Ferdowsian, is the most neglected issue in animal research?

When you burn your finger, the grimace on your face sends a universal message. From Finland to Fiji, virtually any human on earth needs only see your face to know that you're in pain. Facial expressions, anthropologists have long known, are an international language.

But that language, it turns out, isn't exclusive to humans. Mice also express pain through facial expressions—and those grimaces are remarkably similar to yours or mine, according to a recent article published in the journal *Nature Methods*.

In that extremely controversial study, researchers used a wide range of methods to subject mice to various levels of pain. They immersed the animals' tails in hot water, used radiant heat on them, attached a binder clip to their tails, injected irritants into their feet, induced bladder inflammation with a chemical that causes painful cystitis in humans, and injected acetic acid, causing the mice to develop abdominal constriction and writhe. They performed surgery on the mice and did not provide postoperative analgesics.

The study's authors developed a Mouse Grimace Scale as a measurement tool to help quantify the level of pain experienced by mice. They concluded that when subjected to painful stimuli, mice showed discomfort through facial expressions in the same way humans do.

This painful experiment raised many questions among researchers. Criticism of the study was covered in a newsletter called *Laboratory Animal Welfare Compliance* and elsewhere. Critics have maintained that the experiments were cruel and unnecessary.

That study—and the debate surrounding it—highlights critical issues relevant to animal research. For example, mice are now the most commonly used animals in research, but they are not covered by the Animal Welfare Act, one of the few legal protections afforded by U.S. law to other animals used in laboratory experiments.

The original intent of the Laboratory Animal Welfare Act of 1966 was to prevent the unauthorized buying and selling of pet dogs or cats for research purposes. However, the types of enterprises covered, species of animals regulated, reporting requirements, and minimal animal care guidelines were expanded in subsequent amendments.

Inconsistent Regulations

Although those laws provide basic protections for some animals used in research, there are significant inconsistencies among U.S. regulations. For example, more than 90 percent of animals used in research are excluded from the Animal Welfare Act.

The law excludes birds, rats of the genus *Rattus*, mice of the genus *Mus*, and farm animals. Those exclusions are thought to be primarily attributable to the laboratory industry's successful lobbying efforts. In addition, there is no legal threshold for how much pain and suffering an animal can be exposed to in experiments.

Those were some of the issues discussed at a recent conference on animal research and alternatives. My colleagues at the Physicians Committee for Responsible Medicine and I organized "Animals, Research, and Alternatives" to bring together experts with diverse opinions to discuss animal research issues. As a physician concerned about the prevention and alleviation of suffering in both humans and animals, I wanted to help facilitate informed, intelligent discussion about animal research.

Despite well over a century of debate, the ethical and scientific issues surrounding animal research have rarely been studied together in a balanced, organized forum. At our conference, more than 20 speakers shared expertise on the scientific, legal, ethical, and political imperatives regarding animal research.

The first presenter, John Gluck, a professor emeritus of psychology at the University of New Mexico and an affiliate faculty member at Georgetown University's Kennedy Institute of Ethics, set the tone for the conference. After years of conducting primate research, he began studying the ethics of animal research. He and other speakers explained that animals have their own set of needs, and that those needs are compromised when humans use animals in laboratory experiments.

Unlike human research protections, which are now guided by a principled approach, laws governing the use of animals in research have resulted from a largely politicized, patchwork process. That has led to unclear and disparate policies. Meanwhile, studies have dramatically increased our understanding of animal cognition and emotion, suggesting that animals' potential for experiencing harm may be greater than has been appreciated, and that current protections need to be reconsidered.

No Ethical Guidelines

Although today's laws require institutional committee systems to monitor animal research, individuals serving on institutional animal care and use committees have no clear set of ethical principles in which to ground decisions about protocol approval. The scientific question being researched takes precedence over the welfare of the animals. This differs significantly from human research protections, wherein the interests of individuals and populations are protected, sometimes to the detriment of the scientific question.

At the conference, we learned about intriguing advances in medical research, including a surrogate human immune system for predicting vaccine safety, and a revolutionary approach to breast cancer research.

Susan Love, president of the Dr. Susan Love Research Foundation, which focuses on eradicating breast cancer, explained that most breast cancer research in the field is still conducted on animals, even though humans are one of only a few species that develop breast cancer. She discussed the goal of the Army of Women (a partnership between the Avon Foundation for Women and Love's foundation) to challenge research scientists to move from ineffective animal models to breast cancer prevention research conducted on healthy women.

If we could better understand the factors that increase the risk for breast cancer, as well as methods for effective prevention, fewer women would require treatment for breast cancer. But animal experiments do not offer reliable and reproducible findings that can appropriately be applied to women. Whereas animal research is largely investigator initiated, the Army of Women model tries to address the questions that are central to the care of women at risk for or affected by breast cancer. The model has facilitated the recruitment of women for studies such as a national project backed by the National Institutes of Health and the National Institute of Environmental Health to examine how environment and genes affect breast cancer risk. This critical study, which began in 2002, could not have been accomplished with animal research.

William Warren explained a surrogate in vitro human immune system that his company has developed to help predict an individual's immune response to a particular drug or vaccine. The system essentially functions as a clinical trial in a test tube. In other words, it is a virtual human immune system that relies on human immune responses, which differ from those of other animals. The system includes a blood-donor base of hundreds of individuals from diverse populations. It can replace the use of animals for a range of research purposes, most notably vaccine testing. Technologies like those offered by this system could help accelerate the process of developing an HIV vaccine and other immunizations.

Other presenters addressed more of the ethical reasons for moving toward non-animal alternatives. Lori Marino, a senior lecturer in neuroscience and behavioral biology at Emory University, discussed her noninvasive research on dolphin and whale cognition. She described how invasive research involving cetaceans can result in confinement and social deprivation, stress and disease, mortality, and destruction of social cultures. Although both invasive and noninvasive cetacean research attempts to better understand marine animal cognition, Marino's research does not involve medical procedures, such as biopsy darting, or techniques that manipulate the mind, social milieu, or physical freedom of the animals.

Animals Suffer Emotionally

Jaak Panksepp, a neuroscientist at Washington State University, discussed the overwhelming evidence that animals experience basic emotions. For example, mice like to be tickled, much as humans do. If our ears were sufficiently attuned, we could hear their laughter. Marc Bekoff, a professor emeritus of ecology and evolutionary biology at the University of Colorado Boulder, pointed out that the emotional and moral lives of animals matter.

It is now widely acknowledged that animals do suffer, Bekoff explained. Decades of observational and experimental research have provided evidence that animals experience physi-

Beyond Cruelty

Before the Animal Welfare Act, the only laws constraining animal use in society were the anticruelty laws forbidding sadistic, deviant, purposeless, deliberate, unnecessary infliction of pain and suffering on animals, or outrageous neglect. These laws, both by statute and by judicial interpretation, did not apply to socially accepted animal uses such as research or agriculture. . . . The anticruelty laws were only there for society to manage sadists and psychopaths unmoved by self-interest. But with the emergence of new kinds of "normal" animal use—such as intensive agriculture and animal research, both of which caused animal pain and suffering that did not fall under the anticruelty ethic—society was forced to create a new ethic for animals that went "beyond cruelty."

Bernard E. Rollin,
"The Moral Status of Invasive Animal Research,"
Hastings Center Report, *vol. 42, no. 6,*
November–December 2012.

cal pain. Psychological suffering—chronic fear, anxiety, and distress—is another major issue, possibly the most neglected one in animal research.

Perhaps Jeremy Bentham (1748–1832), a legal scholar and social reformer, said it best: "The question is not, 'Can they reason?' nor, 'Can they talk?' but rather, 'Can they suffer?'"

Because animals are sentient beings, they share many qualities with humans. For example, animals demonstrate coordinated responses to pain and many emotional states similar to those of humans. Further, the structures and neuroendocrine mechanisms associated with certain psychiatric conditions are shared across a wide range of animals.

Based on these neuroanatomical and physiological similarities, researchers have described signs of depression in animals, including nonhuman primates, dogs, pigs, cats, birds, and rodents, among others. Learned helplessness, a form of depression that has been described in human patient populations such as victims of domestic violence, has also been identified in rodents, dogs, monkeys, and apes exposed to inescapable shocks. Post-traumatic stress disorder and depression have been described in chimpanzees.

The absence of certain neuroanatomical structures may also be significant because animals with less organized neural circuits may have more limited coping mechanisms useful in reducing the level of pain they feel. Other animal qualities may also be ethically relevant. For example, many animals demonstrate language skills, complex problem-solving abilities, empathy, and self-awareness.

At the conference, I presented my own observational study of chimpanzees. My colleagues and I have found that many chimpanzees who were used in laboratory research continue to exhibit symptoms of depression and post-traumatic stress disorder years after they have been released to sanctuaries.

Chimpanzee Experiments Should End

Because the United States is the last nation conducting large-scale, invasive experiments on chimpanzees, we have to ask ourselves why—particularly when chimpanzee research has hit a dead end for humans. More than two decades of HIV vaccine research using chimpanzees has failed to produce a human vaccine. The story is similar for hepatitis C. Hepatitis behaves very differently in humans than in chimpanzees. Chimpanzees are rarely affected by chronic hepatitis or complications associated with hepatitis, such as cirrhosis or hepatocellular carcinoma. Decades of cancer, malaria, cardiovascular disease, and other forms of research using chimpanzees have led to similar failures.

Meanwhile, chimpanzees have demonstrated their own rich preferences in life, including seeking solitude, experiencing new places, living free from fear of attack, and maintaining lifelong contact with individuals they love.

The subject of animal research is complex. Each of our own opinions has been informed by education, experience, and personal perspective. Conversations surrounding the use of animals in research are understandably truncated by emotion. Often it seems like two sides talking past each other.

It's clear that we're making progress toward replacing the use of animals in invasive experiments, but we have a lot of work ahead of us. I am hopeful that our conference advanced the dialogue and will contribute to scientific and ethical progress for both people and animals.

In years to come, when we have replaced animals in research, future generations will look back and wonder why this advance did not happen sooner. But they will also be thankful for those who improved animals' lives and strove for better, more ethical science.

"Methods excluding animal experimentation are inadequate for understanding the brain's function and disorders."

Alternatives to Animal Experimentation Have Limitations

Max Planck Institute for Biological Cybernetics

The following viewpoint by the Max Planck Institute for Biological Cybernetics explains why alternative methods cannot replace animal experiments in its research on the brain. Although some types of experiments can be done in test tubes, the tissue samples must be obtained by killing animals. Microdosing and computer simulation, which often work for testing drugs, are not applicable to studies of the brain. To simulate something as complex as the brain, says the author, scientists would have to already know most of the details that the research is intended to discover. The Max Planck Institute for Biological Cybernetics is one of eighty-two institutes that make up the Max Planck Society, a prestigious German organization that conducts basic research in various sciences.

As you read, consider the following questions:

1. Why, according to the author, is it necessary to kill animals to do experiments in test tubes?

2. According to the author, why is it not possible to study brain functioning with computer simulations?

3. According to the author, why are more advanced brain scanners unlikely to overcome the limitations of studying brain functioning in humans rather than through animal experiments?

Like most scientists, we embrace alternative methods and employ them in our research whenever possible. Currently available noninvasive methods, however, have their limitations and cannot fully replace animal research.

The methods most frequently propagated by animal research opponents include: in vitro studies, microdosing, computer simulations and functional MRI [magnetic resonance imaging]. In the following, we will take a closer look at each of these methods and their role in cognitive brain research.

In Vitro Experiments

Instead of using living animals, certain experiments can be carried out on tissue samples in a test tube (Latin in vitro, literally "in glass"). However, these preparations cannot regenerate, so they must be acquired by killing animals. Legally, killing an animal to obtain tissue samples is not considered an animal experiment, even if the animal in question is a vertebrate. In contrast, it is regarded as an animal experiment to anesthetize a vertebrate, make observations while the animal is under anesthesia and then to kill the animal by increasing the dose of anesthetic. If good anesthesia practices are employed, the animal will not suffer in either case.

The replacement of in vivo (i.e., living) experiments with in vitro methods does not reduce the number of research animals that are killed. On the contrary, the limited survival time of brain slices, for example, restricts the amount of data that can be obtained from a single experiment.

Microdosing

A 'microdose' is defined as less than one-hundredth of the proposed pharmacological dose up to a maximum of 100 µg. Microdoses of drugs can be measured in any biological sample such as plasma or urine to determine how they are absorbed, distributed, metabolized and excreted (ADME). The analysis is carried out using an accelerator mass spectrometer (AMS). AMS is the most sensitive analytical tool available and is used to study samples from humans, allowing early metabolism data to be obtained before going into human phase 1 trials. By conducting human phase 0 microdosing trials, drug candidates can be efficiently tested right in the relevant species.

Animal research opponents claim that this ultrasensitive analytical technique allows greater predictability than animal studies and reduces the preclinical testing time from 18 months to 6 months. Unfortunately, this particular method is simply not applicable to the neuroanatomical and physiological studies carried out at our institute.

Computer Simulations

Animal research opponents also claim that computer simulations can replace animal experiments. The assumption is that properties of real brains can be inferred from the analysis of artificial neural networks. Unfortunately, this is completely unrealistic, firstly because of the problem of instantiation [assuming that a specific instance typifies a general principle]. Computer simulations themselves teach us that similar functions can be realized by quite different hardware implementations and processing algorithms.

Moreover, it is unclear what kind of "replacement" computers are supposed to be and indeed whether animal experiment opponents really understand computers and computer simulations of neural networks. How can a computer possibly replace recordings from a brain site, for instance? Today's computers, with the existing hardware and operating principles and the hopelessly primitive algorithms and simulations cannot even come close to simulating even the most primitive sensory pathway in a very simple system. They certainly cannot be a substitute for even a small neural population, say, in cortex.

Computer simulations do actually yield acceptable models in research on diabetes, asthma, and drug absorption, although potential new medicines identified using these techniques must still be verified in animal and human tests before licensing.

Other non-animal simulators have been developed for military use to mimic battlefield-induced traumas or to simulate hemorrhaging, fractures, amputations and burns. But all these processes are very many orders of magnitude simpler than the most simplified version of a nucleus in the brain. If we were able to construct artificial models sufficiently similar to their biological counterpart that they could really serve as a substitute for analysis, we would have to know so many details about natural systems that the heuristic value of these models for basic research would be very limited.

When mathematical theories, simulations, and most importantly careful (and mathematically sophisticated) analysis of data are used to support neurobiological research, they can indeed contribute to a certain reduction of animal experimentation. In the same fashion, being able to localize activations and understand the extent of the networks involved in a behavioral task with fMRI [functional magnetic resonance imaging] is immensely without wasting animals and time. Modeling can also contribute to the refinement of working hypotheses and can provide plausibility controls for the interpretation of experimental data. This in turn can serve to optimize experimental protocols and thus to reduce the number of experiments required for the solution of a particular problem. Nonetheless, all of the above are complements to animal experimentation, not substitutes.

Functional MRI in Humans

The main advantages of fMRI lie in its noninvasive nature, ever-increasing availability, relatively high spatiotemporal resolution [precision with regard to location and time], and its capacity to demonstrate the entire network of brain areas engaged when subjects perform particular tasks. . . .

The limitations of fMRI are not related to physics or poor engineering, and they are unlikely to be resolved by increasing the sophistication and power of our scanners; instead, they are due to the circuitry and functional organization of the brain itself, as well as to inappropriate experimental protocols that ignore this organization. . . .

Despite its shortcomings, however, fMRI is currently the best tool we have for gaining insights into brain function and formulating interesting and testable hypotheses, even though the plausibility of these hypotheses critically depends on the magnetic resonance technology being used, the experimental protocol, statistical analysis and insightful modeling. Theories on the brain's functional organization (not just modeling of data) will probably be the best strategy for optimizing all of the above. But hypotheses formulated on the basis of fMRI experiments cannot really be analytically tested with fMRI itself in terms of neural mechanisms, and this is unlikely to change any time in the near future.

Of course, fMRI is not the only methodology that has clear and serious limitations. Electrical measurements of brain activity, including invasive techniques with single or multiple electrodes, also fall short of affording real answers about network activity. Single-unit recordings and firing rates are better suited to the study of cellular properties than of neuronal assemblies, and field potentials share much of the ambiguity discussed in the context of the fMRI signal. None of the above techniques can be a substitute for the others.

Today, a multimodal approach is more necessary than ever for the study of the brain's function and dysfunction. Such an approach will require further improvements to MRI technology and its combination with other noninvasive techniques that directly assess the brain's electrical activity, but it will also require a profound understanding of the neural basis of hemodynamic responses and a tight coupling of human and animal experimentation that will allow us to fathom the homologies between humans and other primates.

Methods excluding animal experimentation are inadequate for understanding the brain's function and disorders. If we really wish to understand how our brain works, we cannot afford to discard any relevant methodology, much less one providing direct information from the actual neural elements that underlie all our cognitive capacities.

> *"Most of these new alternatives that are emerging are coming from the fields of biotechnology, hi-res scanning, and computer science."*

Technological Alternatives Can End the Experimental Use of Animals

George Dvorsky

In the following viewpoint, George Dvorsky argues that putting an end to animal testing is desirable for scientific as well as ethical reasons and that progress is being made toward developing alternatives. Lab-grown cells are being used to predict the toxicity of drugs, chemicals, cosmetics, and other products, he says, and human skin tissue grown in labs is being used for research on the treatment of burns. New human brain scanning technologies are eliminating the need to dissect the brains of living animals. In his opinion, computer simulation of biological processes may someday become accurate enough to eliminate all need for animal testing. Dvorsky is a Canadian bioethicist and futurist. He is the founder and chair of the Rights of Non-Human Persons program at the Institute for Ethics and Emerging Technologies.

As you read, consider the following questions:

1. Why, according to Dvorsky, are most researchers unwilling to stop using mice as subjects of their experiments?

2. With respect to the "three Rs" of animal research, what is meant by refinement?

3. In what technology does Dvorsky believe the future of drug testing lies?

Nobody likes the idea of experimenting on animals. It seems like the definition of inhumanity, especially when you consider the growing evidence that animals have awareness just like us. But there's no doubt that the human race has gained incalculable benefits from the scientific testing of animals. Most scientists don't want to rule out animal testing, because we just don't have any decent alternatives.

Until now. Technology is finally coming up with solutions that could eliminate the practice altogether.

Putting an end to animal experimentation is more than just a matter of ethics. A growing number of scientists and clinicians are challenging the use of animal models on medical and scientific grounds. A 2006 study in *JAMA* [*Journal of the American Medical Association*] concluded that, "patients and physicians should remain cautious about extrapolating the findings of prominent animal research to the care of human disease," and that "even high-quality animal studies will replicate poorly in human clinical research."

Two years ago, independent studies published in *PLOS* [*Biology*] showed that only animal trials with positive results tend to get published, and that only two stroke treatments out of 500 verified that animal models actually worked on humans.

Making matters worse is the fact that mice are used in nearly 60% of all experiments. As *Slate*'s Daniel Engber argues, mice are among the most unreliable test subjects, when it comes to approximating human biological processes. But most scientists are reluctant to move away from this tried-and-true model, mostly because mice are cheap, docile, and good subjects for genetic engineering experiments. They're also denied many of the rights afforded to other animals. Still, Engber points out, "It's not at all clear that the rise of the mouse—and the million research papers that resulted from it—has produced a revolution in public health."

Given these problems, and combined with the overarching ethics question, it's clear that something better has to come along. Thankfully, the process of replacing animal models is largely under way—an effort that began over 50 years ago.

The Three Rs of Animal Testing

Back in 1959, English scientists William Russell and Rex Burch conducted a study to see how animals were being treated at the hands of research scientists. To make their assessments, they looked at the degree of "humaneness" or "inhumaneness" that was afforded to the animals during testing. By analyzing the work being done by scientists in this way, Russell and Burch sought to create a set of guidelines that could be used to reduce the amount of suffering inflicted on laboratory animals.

To that end, they proposed the three Rs of animal testing: Reduction, Refinement, and Replacement.

By practicing reduction, scientists were asked to acquire high-quality data using the smallest possible number of animals. Experiments needed to be designed so that they could continue to yield valuable results, while minimizing (if not eliminating) the need for endless repetition of the same tests. Consequently, scientists were told to work closer with statisticians (to better understand the required level of statistical significance) and to refer to previous studies that had essentially performed the same tests.

Refinement was simply the idea that more humanitarian approaches were required. It was a call to reduce the severity of distress, pain, and fear experienced by many lab animals.

More significantly, however, was the suggestion that scientists replace their lab animals with non-sentient animals—things like microorganisms, metazoan parasites, and certain plants. The less cognitively sophisticated the animal, it was thought, the less capacity it had to experience emotional, physical, and psychological distress.

Since the publication of Russell and Burch's guidelines, a number of scientists and bioethicists have put these policies into practice. But now, as more sophisticated tools emerge, scientists have been given entirely new options for testing—options that will enable them to honor the "R" of replacement.

Technological Alternatives

Most of these new alternatives that are emerging are coming from the fields of biotechnology, hi-res scanning, and computer science.

Take research laboratory CeeTox, for example. They're using human cell-based *in vitro* (lab grown) models to predict the toxicity of drugs, chemicals, cosmetics, and consumer products—tests that are replacing the need to pump potentially hazardous chemicals into animals' stomachs, lungs, and eyes. Likewise, biotech firm Hurel has developed a lab-grown human liver that can be used to break down chemicals. . . .

There's also MatTek's *in vitro* 3-D human skin tissue that's being used by the National Cancer Institute, the U.S military, private companies, and a number of universities. Their virtual skin is proving to be an excellent substitute for the real thing, allowing scientists to conduct burn research, and to test cosmetics, radiation exposure, and so on.

The development of noninvasive brain scanning techniques is also enabling scientists to work on human test subjects.

The Long-Term Debate About Animal Experimentation

The fundamental argument for more than two centuries has been ... that experimenting on animals with the goal of preventing and curing human medical problems was a legitimate addition to the long list of ways in which animals are used for human benefit.

This philosophy has, however, always had its critics. For some individuals, animals should never be viewed simply as objects to be used for human purposes. ... Over time, the idea of animal as object has been replaced in many minds by the concept of animal with value of its own, a principle that has prompted questions about whether or to what extent animals should be subjected to experimentation that is generally not approved for human subjects. ...

For much of the last 150 years, this debate has taken the form of a largely either/or argument: allow or do not allow researchers to use nonhuman animals in their research. Over time, that debate has become more sophisticated and more nuanced. Many people (but certainly not all) accept the fact that animal testing may sometimes be required to answer questions about human health and medical issues. But a wide variety of alternatives to animal testing are now available, and the number of occasions for which animal testing is the only available alternative appears to be becoming smaller and smaller.

David E. Newton,
The Animal Experimentation Debate: A Reference Handbook.
Santa Barbara, CA: ABC-CLIO, 2013.

Technologies such as MRI [magnetic resonance imaging], fMRI [functional magnetic resonance imaging], EEG [electroencephalogram], PET [positron-emission tomography], and CT [computerized tomography] are replacing the need to perform vivisections on the brains of rats, cats, and monkeys.

Likewise, the practice of microdosing, where volunteers are given extremely small onetime drug doses, is allowing researchers to work ethically with humans.

There's also the tremendous potential for computer models—and this is very likely where the future of drug testing and other scientific research lies. And this is a revolution that's already well under way.

The first heart models were developed 13 years ago, kickstarting efforts into the development of simulated lungs, the musculoskeletal system, the digestive system, skin, kidneys, the lymphatic system—and even the brain.

Today, computer simulations are being used to test the efficacy of new medications on asthma, though laws still require that all new drugs get verified in animal and humans tests before licensing. Models are also being used to simulate human metabolism in an effort to predict plaque buildup and cardiovascular risk. These same systems are also being used to evaluate drug toxicity—tests that would have normally involved the use of lab animals. And as we reported a few months ago, new computer simulations can even help scientists predict the negative side effects of drugs. All this is just the tip of the iceberg.

This said, not everyone agrees that computer simulations are the way to go. Some people feel that simulations can never truly paint an accurate picture of what they're trying to model—that it's a classic case of "garbage in, garbage out." The basic reasoning is that scientists can't possibly simulate something they don't truly understand. Consequently, if their models are off by even just a little bit, the entire simulation will diverge dramatically from reality.

But even though these problems are real, they're not necessarily intractable—nor are they deal breakers. It may very well turn out that the margin of error achieved in computer simulations will be comparable (or better) than the current margin of error when testing animal models. And given the rate of technological advance, both in biotechnology and information technology, it's even conceivable that we can simulate the intricate complexity that makes up organisms with extreme accuracy. And at that point, animal experimentation won't even seem like a sensible option.

Periodical and Internet Sources Bibliography

The following articles have been selected to supplement the diverse views presented in this chapter.

Marc Bekoff	"Should Animals Be Used for Scientific or Commercial Testing?," *Animal Emotions— Psychology Today* (blog), October 23, 2013.
Erin Biba	"Animal Testing Is on Its Way Out, Study Says," Salon.com, December 6, 2013.
Helen Briggs	"Human Skin Grown in Lab 'Can Replace Animal Testing,'" BBC News, April 24, 2014.
Tom Chivers	"Animal Testing: Man's Reliance on Rodents Knows No Bounds," *Telegraph* (UK), April 29, 2014.
Richard Conniff	"Should a Vaccine for Wild Chimps Be Tested on Captive Ones?," *Takepart*, May 27, 2014.
John Ericson	"The Price of Killing Off Animal Testing," *Newsweek*, February 20, 2014.
Fiona Fox	"Animal Research Is Brave, Not Cruel, Science," *Guardian* (UK), September 28, 2012.
David Grimm	"How the Rising Status of Cats and Dogs Could Doom Biomedical Research," *Popular Science*, May 21, 2014.
Loren Grush	"New Technology Aims to Minimize Animal Testing for Drug Discovery," FoxNews.com, March 18, 2014.
Joseph Stromberg	"A New Paradigm for Animal Research: Let Them Participate," Smithsonian.com, January 24, 2014.

CHAPTER 4

Are Fraud and Misconduct by Scientists Common?

Chapter Preface

Science is a search for truth, and most people who become scientists are motivated by the desire to seek knowledge. It may seem surprising then that even a small percentage of them turn out to be dishonest. Yet misconduct is a growing problem in science, which is a very competitive field well described by the familiar phrase "publish or perish." A researcher's job security and future project funding depend largely upon the publication of significant results. Scientists are human, and the same failings are found among them as among the rest of the population; so when they lack valid research results to report, some resort to deceit.

Unfortunately, the damage done by scientific fraud can be far-reaching. For instance, in 2009 Scott S. Reuben, an anesthesiologist, was found to have fabricated the results of twenty-one studies of painkillers over more than a decade, some of which he had never even conducted. His false reports had influenced the way doctors treated postsurgical pain, and the effectiveness of that treatment was later questioned. Dr. Reuben eventually pleaded guilty and was sentenced to jail for health care fraud, but that did little for the patients who may have suffered harm. Most scientific fraud does not have such a direct effect on the public, but it invalidates the premises upon which other scientists base their work, and it also results in the waste of a great deal of money.

According to the Office of Research Integrity (ORI), the agency of the US Department of Health and Human Services that investigates reports of misconduct by scientists who receive federal funds, "Research misconduct means fabrication, falsification, or plagiarism in proposing, performing, or reviewing research, or in reporting research results." Obviously it is fraudulent to fabricate—that is, to make up fake data—or to falsify, which means to manipulate an experiment or data from it in such a way as to give a false impression of the results. For example, this is sometimes done by omitting statistical data that conflict with the desired conclusion or by altering images with Photoshop.

A much more common form of misconduct is plagiarism. This term covers more than simply copying someone else's words without putting them in quotation marks, although that happens all too often. It also includes using another person's ideas or research results without giving credit to that person either in the text or in footnotes. In addition, for scientists self-plagiarism—using the same words or data analysis in more than one publication to get duplicate credit for the same work—is also considered misconduct.

In addition to these types of misconduct, which are the most serious, there are many others. Ghost authorship is the practice of putting one's name on a paper when he or she is not the actual author. Sometimes researchers merely do not want to do the work; other times they allow their names to lend credibility to reports by others such as drug companies. Senior researchers sometimes take credit for work by their students or subordinates. Another dishonest act is the failure to report the results of an experiment if they were negative. This not only gives a wrong impression that the scientist is always successful but also misleads other researchers who are working in the same field. Misconduct also occurs when scientists fail to disclose conflict of interest, such as a financial connection with a drug company, which might bias their interpretation of their experiments. Furthermore, conducting clinical studies without approval and the informed consent of subjects is highly unethical.

Although scientific misconduct is inexcusable, opinions vary as to how frequently it occurs and what effect it has on the public's perception of science. The authors in this chapter present differing views of these issues.

"A review of retractions in medical and biological peer-reviewed journals finds the percentage of studies withdrawn because of fraud or suspected fraud has jumped substantially."

Scientific Research Fraud Is on the Rise

Associated Press

In the following viewpoint, the Associated Press reports on a study that found fraudulent publications by scientists are more common than they used to be. A large percentage of retractions of scientific papers have occurred because of fraud. The author partially attributes this to an increase in deception throughout society. Although few scientists commit fraud, its reach has a greater effect than other forms of deception because scientists commit fraud in important areas where people can be hurt by wrong information and because fraud causes the public to lose faith in science.

As you read, consider the following questions:

1. What type of misconduct other than fraud did the study find had caused scientific papers to be retracted?

2. What prominent research concerning vaccines was retracted because of fraud?

3. According to the author of the study on fraud, why are
   scientists tempted to cheat?

Fraud in scientific research, while still rare, is growing at a troubling pace, a new study finds.

A review of retractions in medical and biological peer-reviewed journals finds the percentage of studies withdrawn because of fraud or suspected fraud has jumped substantially since the mid-1970s. In 1976, there were fewer than 10 fraud retractions for every 1 million studies published, compared with 96 retractions per million in 2007.

The study authors aren't quite sure why this is happening. But they and outside experts point to pressure to hit it big in science, both for funding and attention, and to what seems to be a subtle increase in deception in overall society that science may simply be mirroring.

Fraud in life sciences research is still minuscule and committed by only a few dozen scientific scofflaws. However, it causes big problems, said Arturo Casadevall, a professor of microbiology at the Albert Einstein College of Medicine in New York. Casadevall is the lead author of the study which looked at the reasons for 2,047 retractions among many millions of studies published in journals and kept in a government database for medically focused research.

Fraud was the No. 1 cause of retractions, accounting for 43 percent of them. When fraud was combined with other areas of misconduct, such as plagiarism, it explained about 2 out of 3 retractions, the study found.

"Very few people are doing it, but when they do it, they are doing it in areas that are very important," Casadevall said. "And when these things come out, society loses faith in science."

Prominent retractions that Casadevall cited for fraud include a notorious British study that wrongly linked childhood vaccines to autism, nine separate studies on highly touted research at Duke University about cancer treatment, and work by a South Korean cloning expert who later was convicted in court of embezzlement and illegally buying human eggs for research.

Casadevall said he was surprised because he didn't set out to study fraud. His plan was to examine the most common avoidable errors that caused retractions. What he found was that 889 of the more than 2,000 retractions were due to fraud or suspected fraud.

While other studies have shown a rise in retractions, no previous study has found scientific misconduct as the leading cause, said Nicholas Steneck, director of the research ethics [and integrity] program at the University of Michigan, who wasn't involved in the Casadevall study. That shows a need for better, more honest reporting of retractions by the science journals themselves, he said.

He and others also said the findings suggest there may just be better detection of scientific fraud overall.

Most "scientists out there are well meaning and honest people who are going to be totally appalled by this," Casadevall said.

The study was published online Monday in the *Proceedings of the National Academy of Sciences* [PNAS], which had the second-most retracted articles for all reasons, behind only the journal *Science*.

The publication with the most fraud-based retractions was the *Journal of Biological Chemistry*. PNAS ranked fifth.

Pressure to Cheat

Casadevall said that even if society as a whole has become more deceptive, "I used to think that science was on a differ-

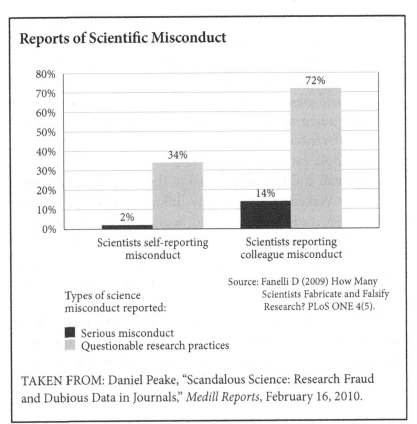

Reports of Scientific Misconduct

Types of science misconduct reported:

Source: Fanelli D (2009) How Many Scientists Fabricate and Falsify Research? PLoS ONE 4(5).

■ Serious misconduct
▢ Questionable research practices

TAKEN FROM: Daniel Peake, "Scandalous Science: Research Fraud and Dubious Data in Journals," *Medill Reports*, February 16, 2010.

ent plane. But I think science is like everybody else and that we are susceptible to the same pressures."

In science, he said, "there's a disproportionate reward system" so if a researcher is published in certain prominent journals they are more likely to get jobs and funding, so the temptations increase.

"Bigger money makes for bigger reasons for fraud," said New York University bioethicist Arthur Caplan. "More fame, more potential for profit. . . Some of the cheating and fraud is not too dissimilar to the cheating and fraud we've seen in banking."

Science historian Marcel LaFollette, author of a book about science fraud *Stealing into Print*, said researchers can't prove that more people are lying in general in society, but they get the distinct feeling it's happening more. And in 2006 an Associated Press-Ipsos poll found that while most people say they don't approve of lying, 65 percent of those questioned said it is OK to lie in certain situations.

The world has become accustomed to lying and forgives politicians when they do it in relationships, LaFollette said. But it's different when it's a doctor, scientist or an engineer because people can get hurt, she said.

Casadevall and Caplan pointed to the 1998 study in *Lancet* by Andrew Wakefield temporarily linking childhood vaccines to autism—a study later retracted because it was found to be what another scientific journal called "an elaborate fraud."

"Think about the damage society took when mothers started to question vaccines," Casadevall said. "That's damage and it's still going on."

Reached at home in Texas, Wakefield, who was banned from practicing medicine in his native Great Britain and whose claims are contrary to what prevailing established medical research shows about vaccine and autism, said: "There was no fraud and to use this and to use me as a poster child of fraud really compounds that error."

Casadevall said his work is about science trying to clean its own house. And because it's about fraud, he said he did one extra thing with his study: He sent reviewers not just a summary of their work, but all the data, "so they can check on us."

> "Cases of scientific misconduct are extremely rare, which is probably why they are so highly publicized when they occur."

Scientific Misconduct Occurs but Is Rare

Richard B. Primack

In the following viewpoint, Richard B. Primack points out that although recent cases of scientific misconduct reported in the press might lead readers to assume that such misconduct is widespread, in his opinion this is not the case. He has seen only one case of fraud in nine years of editing the journal Biological Conservation, *he says, and a study of retractions has shown that they are extremely rare. He states that he has encountered a few papers with ethical problems not serious enough to be defined as misconduct but maintains that the vast majority of researchers have high ethical standards. Primack is a professor of biology at Boston University, editor in chief of the journal* Biological Conservation, *and the author of two textbooks.*

As you read, consider the following questions:

1. About how many of ten thousand scientific papers are retracted, according to the study reported by Primack?

2. Why does Primack think that the specific case he describes, in which scientists copied sentences from a similar paper, should not be considered serious misconduct?

3. What problems does Primack mention concerning misconduct by reviewers rather than by authors?

In a recent issue of *Biological Conservation*, the authors of a paper published in 2011 describe that certain results from their paper need to be removed. The reason for this, as described by the authors, is that the data provided by one of the coauthors could not be verified, as determined following an official investigation by their university. Readers of this journal and other scientific journals might be concerned that this example and others reported in the press and scientific outlets suggest that scientific misconduct may be both widespread and increasing, perhaps due to increasing competition for jobs and research funding. However, we at *Biological Conservation* come to a very different conclusion. In fact, this is the first case of serious scientific misconduct that we have seen over the past 9 years of the journal, during which time around 2,000 papers have been published. Consequently it appears that scientific misconduct in this area of biology is actually quite rare. In fact, analysis by [R.G.] Steen suggests that retractions of scientific papers occur at a rate of 1–3 papers per 10,000 published. It is also possible that there are undetected cases of misconduct that were never uncovered.

However, we think that over the years, these would have been discovered if they existed. A careful reader will note that we used the words "serious misconduct" in the previous paragraph. We did this deliberately as we have encountered a small number of papers that present ethical issues, but fall somewhat short of real scientific misconduct. For example, we have had two cases in which an author submits a paper analyzing data and another scientist writes to us that the author does not have permission to use this data. In both of these examples, the authors have asserted that they do have proper permission.

We requested that the authors and other interested parties resolve this issue to everyone's satisfaction before we considered the papers for publication. In both cases this appeared to work.

In a second example, we learned that a paper published by European authors had many sentences of its Materials and Methods and Results sections taken directly from a very similar paper, but on different species, by an earlier author, whom the European authors cited. When contacted, the European authors asserted that since their paper was so similar in approach to the earlier paper, it was acceptable to use the same language, especially since they had cited the earlier paper. When we pointed out that this was plagiarism of another scientist's words, even if cited, the European authors agreed to write a letter of apology that the earlier author graciously accepted.

And as a third example, in the process of reviewing a paper in environmental economics, a reviewer pointed out the paper had been published already in an online university journal. The authors had not mentioned this in their cover letter, and had even stated that their paper had never been published previously. While we understand that the publishing practices in the field of economics are quite different from biology and other branches of science, we felt that the authors had not been transparent and honest about their paper. We rejected their paper, largely due to poor reviews, but we also informed the authors that their behavior was inappropriate for a biological journal even if it was acceptable in economics.

There have also been a number of cases in which authors have felt that reviewers have acted in an unethical manner. In

Research Misconduct

Research misconduct is defined as fabrication, falsification, or plagiarism in proposing, performing, or reviewing research or in reporting research results, according to "Public Health Service Policies on Research Misconduct."

- *Fabrication* is defined as making up data or results and recording or reporting them.
- *Falsification* is defined as manipulating research materials, equipment, or processes or changing or omitting data or results such that the research is not accurately represented in the research record.
- *Plagiarism* is defined as appropriating another person's ideas, processes, results, or words without giving appropriate credit.

A finding of research misconduct requires the following:

- There must be a significant departure from accepted practices of the relevant research community.
- The misconduct must be committed intentionally, knowingly, or recklessly.
- The allegation must be proven by a preponderance of the evidence.

Research misconduct does not include honest error or differences of opinion. All institutions receiving PHS [Public Health Service] funding must have written policies and procedures for addressing allegations of research misconduct.

*"NIH Policies and Procedures for
Promoting Scientific Integrity," National Institutes
of Health Office of the Director, November 2012.*

one paper, the authors stated that a reviewer was threatening physical violence and may have been engaged in inappropriate cyber-stalking.

In another paper, the author asserted that the two reviewers were deliberately trying to wreck his career. We carefully investigated these charges, but we did not find any evidence for the accusations.

In summary, considering the approximately 2,000 papers that we have published in recent years, and the roughly 8,000 papers that we have received and reviewed, this present case of scientific misconduct is not at all representative. Such cases of scientific misconduct are extremely rare, which is probably why they are so highly publicized when they occur. While we at *Biological Conservation* continue to be concerned and vigilant over the issue of scientific misconduct, we also remain impressed by the high ethical standards of the vast majority of the scientific community, including both authors and reviewers.

"Science reporters now have a significant role in investigating scientific misconduct."

Reporting of Scientific Misconduct Should Go Beyond High-Profile Scandals

Declan Fahy

In the following viewpoint, Declan Fahy argues that cases of scientific misconduct should not be dismissed as isolated behavior, as they often are. Although scientists have traditionally done this, he says, misconduct is less exceptional than many would like to believe. In his opinion, science journalists should not confine their reporting to high-profile scandals but should expose the low-level misconduct that is all too frequent. They should also cover retractions of scientific papers, in which the authors admit their wrongdoing, and they should point out the sociological pressures that contribute to the problem. Fahy is an assistant professor in the School of Communication at American University in Washington, DC.

As you read, consider the following questions:

1. When, according to Fahy, did scientific misconduct first get public attention?

Declan Fahy, "Rooting Out Bad Science," *Columbia Journalism Review*, May 23, 2013. www.cjr.org. Copyright © 2013 by the Columbia Journalism Review. All rights reserved. Reproduced with permission.

2. According to the study reported by Fahy, what percentage of scientists admits to having engaged in serious misconduct at least once?

3. According to the experts Fahy quotes, what would be a better way of judging scientific misconduct than consideration of high-profile cases?

The extraordinary case of academic fraudster Diederick Stapel followed the typical narrative of a scientific scandal.

A professor of social psychology at Tilburg University, he became a star researcher in his native Netherlands and abroad after years of eye-catching experiments on human behavior, such as a 2011 study published in *Science* that found a rubbish-strewn environment brought out racist behaviors in people.

But in October 2011, after Stapel's colleagues and graduate students told university authorities that they suspected he was making up results, an initial investigation revealed that he had committed substantial research fraud since at least 2004 in what currently stands at more than 50 of his papers. The university suspended Stapel, but keeping with the standard scandal narrative, a final report on the affair, released last fall, wrote him off as a lone careerist, although it did note that some of his coauthors should have been more critical. Unfortunately, this tendency to treat misconduct as isolated behavior is all too common.

The historian of science Marcel LaFollette has noted that initially, when faced with scientific impropriety, scientists around the world tend to present a variation on this enduring story line. As she explained in a 2000 article for *Experimental Biology and Medicine*, "They have characterized the offender as aberrant, argued that the episode is isolated, or attempted to explain it as caused by stress, bad judgment, or moral corruption (or all three)."

However, as Yudhijit Bhattacharjee noted in an unflinching 6,400-word examination of the Stapel affair in *The New York Times Magazine* in April, Stapel's exceptional case needs to be considered against a background where "at the very least ... the number of bad actors in science isn't as insignificant as many would like to believe."

The Role of Science Journalism

Science reporters now have a significant role in investigating scientific misconduct. Until the 1970s, LaFollette noted, cases of scientific misconduct were resolved quietly within a laboratory or an institution. The first case to get significant public attention, she wrote, was the 1974 case of William T. Summerlin, who fraudulently claimed to have transplanted skin between mice. But when general and science reporters focused increasingly on cases of fraud, political attention followed and scientific misconduct became a public policy issue.

Today, science journalists can continue to perform this important function, but should go beyond the high-profile scandals to reveal an underreported aspect of contemporary research—the low-level misconduct that corrodes the scientific enterprise.

A 2009 *PLOS ONE* study by Dr. Daniele Fanelli, a researcher at the University of Edinburgh who studies bias and misconduct in science, found that two percent of scientists, on average, admitted to at least one incident of serious misconduct, such as fabrication, falsification or modification of data—all of which distort scientific knowledge. When talking about their colleagues' behavior, 14 percent said they observed serious scientific misconduct.

In this climate, there are several ways that science journalists can enhance their reporting, and consequently, public understanding, of misconduct. The first step is to make this problematic aspect of the scientific culture explicit, as Carl

© Benita Epstein Cartoons.

Zimmer did in his detailed examination of how pressures to achieve and maintain success have fueled an increasing rate of scientific retractions, which ran last year in *The New York Times*.

Another way to do this is for reporters to cover retractions, the public admissions by journals that studies they printed should never have been published, most often because of deliberate deceit or honest mistakes. This is routine practice at Reuters Health, for example, according to Ivan Oransky, its executive editor. Moreover, he said that if a reporter covered a paper that was retracted, they would update their earlier report. "When we do it on a five- or six-year-old study, we can look a little silly," he said. "But we'll take a little looking silly, if it corrects the record."

Oransky is also cofounder, with Adam Marcus, of Retraction Watch, which since 2010 has chronicled the steady stream of retractions from scientific journals. Oransky hopes that the site not only documents these admissions of error or misconduct, but also has an agenda-setting role in a new science journalism ecosystem, serving as a source for stories upon which other journalists follow up.

The Significance of Social Forces

At another level, journalists can report on the sociological aspects of science that contribute to misconduct. "A simple thing to remember is that scientists are human," said Oransky. But he said the way some science stories are written drains this human element out of the process. Missing are descriptions of what it "takes to publish a paper, the pressure to cut corners, the competition." Oransky noted that by "focusing on the outlier, such as Stapel, one forgets that there are forces that can warp or skew the work of even the best-intentioned of scientists."

To help understand these social and cultural forces, reporters can read the work of prominent researchers who have highlighted problematic features of science. Essential readings include the provocative 2005 *PLOS Medicine* essay by the Stanford medical professor John Ioannidis, "Why Most Published Research Findings Are False," that examined the consequences of scientific bias. Another crucial text is the 2011 editorial in *Infection and Immunity* by University of Washington medical professor Ferric Fang that called for methodological and cultural reforms for a scientific community that is showing "signs of dysfunction," including a winner-takes-all culture, where researchers race to publish in the most prominent journals and compete for grant funding.

At the same time, journalists can offer some proportion about the scale of misconduct. Fanelli noted that the rising rate of retractions is usually the only evidence presented to demonstrate increased levels of scientific misconduct. But he said: "There was no culture of retracting papers until recently. Too often, the high rate of retractions is taken to point to a problem. That is a mistake." He said that while most retractions currently occur because a journal has been alerted to or discovered some form of misconduct, retractions can be viewed more positively, as an example of scientists voluntarily cleaning up the scientific record. Science, said Fanelli, "would also benefit from having more researchers retracting their mistakes spontaneously, and more journals ensuring efficient retractions."

And others caution against generalizing too much from particular high-profile cases. "It is important to not judge the scientific discipline where these cases occur because of the misguided actions of a few individuals," Jeff Spies, codirector of the Center for Open Science, which aims in part to make science more transparent, wrote in an email. "If the discipline's to be judged, it should be by how the community responds. I would like to see a focus on the very positive side of these cases, and that is how the scientific community comes together to address the underlying issues rather than hiding or ignoring them." (For a well-reasoned explanation of how psychology is correcting itself, see this *New Yorker* piece by Gary Marcus headlined, "The Crisis in Social Psychology That Isn't.")

Particular scientific scandals make compelling stories. But reporters can paint a bigger picture of the scientific enterprise, revealing, rather than obscuring, the social environment in which scientists work. It is a culture in which, wrote Fang, to "be successful, today's scientists must often be self-promoting entrepreneurs whose work is driven not only by curiosity but by personal ambition, political concerns, and quests for funding." To fully comprehend the Stapel case, it is a culture readers need to understand.

> "Reports [of scientific misconduct] are more an example of sensationalist media latching on to a hot topic than a true account of the deterioration of scientific values."

Scientific Misconduct Is Less Common than Implied by the Media

Heinrich Rohrer

In the following viewpoint, Heinrich Rohrer declares that although the media have created the impression that scientific misconduct has become widespread, in reality it is a rare exception and has not interfered with scientific progress. Nevertheless, he says, the scientific community should pursue such cases, and furthermore, it should question the current practice of fostering pressure for scientists to publish more and more studies in the pursuit of recognition—incentives that lead to the misconduct that does exist. Rohrer received the Nobel Prize in physics in 1986.

As you read, consider the following questions:

1. What, according to Rohrer, is at stake when the scientific community fails to crack down on scientific misconduct?

2. Why, in Rohrer's opinion, is there less misconduct in "hard" sciences such as mathematics and physics than in other types of science?

3. What sort of current research activities does Rohrer feel should not be called "science"?

Scientific fraud, plagiarism, and ghost writing are increasingly being reported in the news media, creating the impression that misconduct has become a widespread and omnipresent evil in scientific research. But these reports are more an example of sensationalist media latching on to a hot topic than a true account of the deterioration of scientific values.

Far from being the norm in scientific research, fraud and cheating are rare exceptions and are usually quickly identified by other scientists. And the public seems to understand this. Indeed, trust and confidence in scientific research have not been seriously undermined by reports of misconduct. Nor have these rare incidents curtailed scientific progress, which is so valuable to humankind.

To be sure, even a few cases of scientific misconduct are too many. Scientists are expected to be beacons of hope in the search for knowledge—and clever enough not to try to get away with cheating. Preventive mechanisms are in place to hold responsible the few who take the gamble. But, while the scientific community—including academic and professional institutions, agency heads, managers, and editors—is often reluctant to handle cases of misconduct rigorously, the reputation of science as a whole is at stake, not just that of a person, institution, journal, or national science entity.

Ironically, those who are caught often blame their misconduct on competition, pressure to publish, and recognition and prizes—the very practices and incentives that the scientific community introduced and fostered. Indeed, while the menace of misconduct has been exaggerated, we have to rethink how we conduct science—its values, virtues, and shortcomings.

Scientists must follow a path that is not scientifically predefined, and that requires decisions at every step. Whether they are right or wrong becomes clear in retrospect, which is why errors are unavoidable (though they should not be left uncorrected for long). Science means constantly walking a tightrope between blind faith and curiosity; between expertise and creativity; between bias and openness; between experience and epiphany; between ambition and passion; and between arrogance and conviction—in short, between an old today and a new tomorrow.

The Problems with How Science Is Conducted

But, nowadays, research increasingly is misdirected toward lucrative prizes, professional recognition, and financial gains—rewards that are suffocating the creativity and passion that scientific progress demands. As T.S. Eliot put it, "Where is the wisdom we have lost in knowledge? Where is the knowledge we have lost in information?"

In the "hard" sciences, such as mathematics and physics, the truth can be established more transparently, making these fields less prone to scientific misconduct. But branches like medicine, humanities, philosophy, economics, and other social sciences, which rely more heavily on openness and imagination, can be manipulated more easily to suit the goals of bureaucrats.

Indeed, today, too many areas that are being called "science"—for example, collecting biased statistics in order to

Why Ethics in Research Is Important

There are several reasons why it is important to adhere to ethical norms in research. First, norms promote the aims of research, such as knowledge, truth, and avoidance of error. For example, prohibitions against fabricating, falsifying, or misrepresenting research data promote the truth and avoid error. Second, since research often involves a great deal of cooperation and coordination among many different people in different disciplines and institutions, ethical standards promote the values that are essential to collaborative work, such as trust, accountability, mutual respect, and fairness. For example, many ethical norms in research, such as guidelines for authorship, copyright and patenting policies, data-sharing policies, and confidentiality rules in peer review, are designed to protect intellectual property interests while encouraging collaboration. . . . Third, many of the ethical norms help to ensure that researchers can be held accountable to the public. . . . Fourth, ethical norms in research also help to build public support for research. People are more likely to fund research projects if they can trust the quality and integrity of research. Finally, many of the norms of research promote a variety of other important moral and social values, such as social responsibility, human rights, animal welfare, compliance with the law, and health and safety. . . . A researcher who fabricates data in a clinical trial may harm or even kill patients, and a researcher who fails to abide by regulations and guidelines relating to radiation or biological safety may jeopardize his health and safety or the health and safety of staff and students.

David B. Resnik,
"What Is Ethics in Research & Why Is It Important?"
National Institute of Environmental Health Services,
May 1, 2011.

make a politician's (or corporation's) point, or publishing a variation of existing knowledge—fall far short of scientific standards of originality and the quest for basic insight.

And yet, while bureaucratization of science has fueled concerns about its attractiveness to talented thinkers, we should not be overly pessimistic. To be sure, many people have lamented the loss of brilliant minds to the financial sector over the past few decades. But perhaps we should consider it a stroke of luck that these geniuses created their mess somewhere else.

Moreover, we underestimate the younger generation of scientists. Like the previous generation, many gifted young researchers know that they must work hard to meet monumental challenges and make valuable contributions to society.

But we must be careful not to corrupt their work with the questionable practices that the scientific community has adopted in recent years. The new generation of researchers must be given the skills and values—not just scientific ideals, but also awareness of human weaknesses—that will enable it to correct its forebears' mistakes.

> *"Scientists and editors are pushing universities and research agencies to take more responsibility for investigating and punishing misconduct."*

Scientific Misconduct: More Cops, More Robbers?

Colin Macilwain

In the following viewpoint, Colin Macilwain reports that because of recent high-profile cases of scientific misconduct, scientists around the world are taking it more seriously than in the past and are attempting to investigate it more thoroughly. However, he says, it is uncertain whether the number of cases reported is representative of the number that occur, which studies suggest is much larger than reported. Moreover, investigating agencies deal only with the most serious forms of misconduct, and research integrity is perceived differently in different cultures, a situation that has international impact. Macilwain is the editor of Research Europe *and associate editor of* Research Fortnight.

As you read, consider the following questions:

1. What forms of scientific misconduct are referred to by the acronym FFP?

2. What type of scientific research is under the jurisdiction of the Office of Research Integrity (ORI)?

3. According to Macilwain, what factors are causing fear that the amount of scientific misconduct is likely to increase?

In the past year, there has been an upsurge in global activity to address research misconduct. Scientists and editors are pushing universities and research agencies to take more responsibility for investigating and punishing misconduct. Canada has put new procedures in place to do this, and other nations are under pressure to follow suit.

Two main factors are likely driving this upsurge in official activity. One is the drip-drip-drip of high-profile misconduct cases. In 2005, Seoul National University unmasked the fraud by the Korean stem cell biologist, Hwang Woo-suk, who had reported the successful production of human embryonic stem cells by cloning. Two years later, the Intergovernmental Panel on Climate Change erroneously reported false claims that all Himalayan glaciers would likely melt by 2035. Then, in 2010, the contentious research of Andrew Wakefield—which advocated a link between autism and the measles, mumps, and rubella vaccine—was discredited when the UK [United Kingdom] General Medical Council convicted him of misconduct and questioned the content of his papers.

A second factor is the flood of hard information regarding the frequency of misconduct. The caseload of the ORI [Office of Research Integrity] has approximately doubled over the last decade, during which time the total number of retractions in scientific literature has risen tenfold, reaching approximately 400 last year. The emerging subdiscipline of research into research integrity (RRI) has built up a body of evidence that "serious misconduct," generally classified as "falsification, fabrication, and plagiarism (FFP)" is more frequent than these numbers suggest and that shaded forms of misconduct, such as redundant publication and the suppression of negative results, are much more common again.

Still, the scale of the problem remains open to dispute. In 2010, ORI was notified of 288 misconduct allegations, inquiries, and investigations. It also opened 28 of its own investigations. ORI deals only with research supported by the US Department of Health and Human Services (e.g., the National Institutes of Health [NIH]), and other US agencies probably encounter a similar caseload. Canada investigates approximately 20 cases per year, and the UK Research Integrity Office (UKRIO) receives about one inquiry per week from universities seeking advice, according to its director, James Parry.

But what fraction of scientific misconduct cases do these numbers represent? "It's tough to know if you're looking at the tip of the iceberg or the bottom of the iceberg," says Mark Frankel, director of scientific responsibility, human rights, and law at the American Association for the Advancement of Science (AAAS). However, the research in this field, the best of which relies on self-reporting questionnaires that researchers post anonymously, suggests that it is the tip of the iceberg.

According to a widely quoted 2009 metastudy by Daniele Fanelli of the University of Edinburgh, approximately 2% of researchers confess to FFP, and as many as one-third confess to lesser forms of misconduct. Fanelli, an evolutionary biologist who now studies research conduct, says the work has been surprisingly well received by other scientists. "One of the things that has made misconduct less of a taboo is the fact that researchers are studying it, the same way that they would study anything else."

These trends have shifted the way in which the issue is perceived by scientists. "The community's approach has really changed," says Frankel. "They were in denial for many years: but now, with twenty or thirty people being found guilty of misconduct each year, researchers realize that there is a problem."

Minor Misconducts Forecast Fraud?

Around the world, a small cadre of university and government officials is charged with containing this problem. ORI is the global leader in this field; with a nine million dollar budget and a staff of 30, it requires annual certification from some 5,000 institutions worldwide. It also oversees their investigations, taking them on itself when necessary. But ORI's staff has slipped from 50 a decade ago, and it lacked a full-time director from 2009 until this January, when David Wright, a historian of science and former research integrity officer at Michigan State University, took on the role.

Wright says that there has been a shift during the past decade for ORI investigators to be more "friendly and supportive" toward the university integrity officers whose work they supervise. He says he wants its staff to work hand in hand with research institutions to strengthen both their investigations and their training programs.

But ORI's reach is limited to publicly funded health research; it has no jurisdiction over privately or foundation-funded research, even when most of this takes place in the same laboratories as NIH work. And its regime doesn't extend to other public funding agencies, who work by different rules. The National Science Foundation, for example, differs from ORI in that it doesn't publicly identify those who it finds guilty of misconduct.

Most importantly, federal agencies concern themselves with only the narrowest definition of research misconduct: FFP. That decision was made by the White House back in 2000, after scientific organizations successfully fought off recommendations of an independent commission, which was headed by Ken Ryan of Harvard University.

Ryan called for a broader definition of "misconduct" that included suppressing data and mistreating staff. But research organizations argued that FFP was fundamentally distinct from these lesser offenses.

The Woo-suk case, however, appeared to vindicate Ryan's approach. Before Woo-suk was accused of data fabrication, it was reported that he had used his laboratory assistants as sources for difficult-to-obtain human eggs—a serious accusation that senior colleagues regarded as incidental to his work. Only later did it emerge that he was fabricating data, too. His two main papers were retracted by *Science* in 2006.

That illustrated Ryan's basic point: if you're crassly exploiting female students, for example, the government probably shouldn't be paying for your work.

The United States has nonetheless stuck with the more narrow definition: falsification, fabrication, and plagiarism. But it is the only major power to do so. "The US system is the oldest," observes Nicholas Steneck, a research integrity specialist at the University of Michigan, "but I wouldn't call it the most advanced. What limits it is that its definition of misconduct is so narrow, and it is limited to government-funded research." . . .

International Arms Race

Additional problems are raised by stark variation in how research integrity is perceived in different cultures. German courts, for example, have been reluctant to sanction the idea that a university or state agency can tell an individual researcher what to do.

Last August, the *FASEB Journal* retracted a 2003 paper by the German neuroscientist Nicolai Savaskan. The US journal had received a letter from Savaskan's university, the Charité- [Charité–University Medicine Berlin] in Berlin, stating that his paper contained "gross flaws." Savaskan sued the university and won. That particular verdict was overturned on appeal in May.

Endocrinologist Volker Bähr, who was appointed as Germany's first-ever research integrity officer at Charité last summer, says that the legacy of Nazism has left the courts generally inclined to place free expression above any institution's right to sanction scientists. "As a consequence, it is often difficult to rectify scientific misconduct," Bähr says.

Such international variations are now being investigated by the InterAcademy Council (IAC), which represents the national academies—the self-governing clubs of very senior scientists that "speak for science" around the world. The IAC's study into "research integrity and scientific responsibility" was prompted, in part, by the damage that the Himalayan glacier claim did to the global reputation of the whole IPCC, says Robbert Dijkgraff, a physicist and president of the Royal Netherlands Academy [of Arts and Sciences] who also cochairs the IAC. "Misconduct by one scientist in country X can undermine public confidence in country Y," he says. "The thing we got worried about is where research happens in large international collaborations—so that the weakest link determines the outcome."

The IAC panel will report this summer and hopes that its findings will help universities, agencies, and governments around the world to better manage research misconduct. The organization also plans to produce sets of training material by next year. Dijkgraff, who becomes director of the Institute for Advanced Study in Princeton in July, thinks that better training holds the key. "We don't teach our young people enough sense of the enormous responsibility that they have, or of the consequences of misconduct," he says.

The Internet, Photoshop, cutthroat competition, and even internationalism all lead pessimists to fear that research misconduct can only increase. At the same time, parts of the community are taking the problem seriously and are proactively pushing for more government action and funding to clamp down hard on it.

"There's broad recognition of the scope of the problem and agreement that it is underreported. It is being handled better, by and large," says Wright. "But there are also more and more ways for people who want to cheat to do so—and lack of funding will induce more of them to try." The result, the ORI director notes, is a battle between two conflicting dynamics that isn't going to end anytime soon. "It's like an arms race," he asserts.

VIEWPOINT 6

> "High-profile examples have exposed a greyer area of bad or lazy scientific practice that many had preferred to brush under the carpet."

Fraud and Misconduct Are Threatening Scientific Research

Alok Jha

In the following viewpoint, Alok Jha discusses the recent increase in scientific misconduct, the reasons it occurs, and the difficulty in dealing with it. He describes several of the most prominent cases in which scientists falsified their data and how this fraud was discovered. Sometimes, he says, false data can do serious harm, especially in the field of medicine; yet fraud is difficult to detect. He points out that since society has to rely on science, it is important for scientists to be trusted and for them to be able to trust one another's work. Jha is a science correspondent for the British national newspaper the Guardian.

As you read, consider the following questions:

1. What are some forms of scientific misconduct that are less serious than plagiarism, fabrication, and falsification of research?

2. Who is responsible for investigating and punishing scientific misconduct?

3. Why, according to Jha, is it difficult for scientists who try to replicate and confirm others' research to get negative results published?

Dirk Smeesters had spent several years of his career as a social psychologist at Erasmus University in Rotterdam studying how consumers behaved in different situations. Did colour have an effect on what they bought? How did death-related stories in the media affect how people picked products? And was it better to use supermodels in cosmetics adverts than average-looking women?

The questions are certainly intriguing, but unfortunately for anyone wanting truthful answers, some of Smeesters' work turned out to be fraudulent. The psychologist, who admitted "massaging" the data in some of his papers, resigned from his position in June after being investigated by his university, which had been tipped off by Uri Simonsohn from the University of Pennsylvania in Philadelphia. Simonsohn carried out an independent analysis of the data and was suspicious of how perfect many of Smeesters' results seemed when, statistically speaking, there should have been more variation in his measurements.

The case, which led to two scientific papers being retracted, came on the heels of an even bigger fraud, uncovered last year, perpetrated by the Dutch psychologist Diederik Stapel. He was found to have fabricated data for years and published it in at least 30 peer-reviewed papers, including a report in the journal *Science* about how untidy environments may encourage discrimination.

The cases have sent shockwaves through a discipline that was already facing serious questions about plagiarism. . . .

Cases of scientific misconduct tend to hit the headlines precisely because scientists are supposed to occupy a moral high ground when it comes to the search for truth about nature. The scientific method developed as a way to weed out human bias. But scientists, like anyone else, can be prone to bias in their bid for a place in the history books.

Massaged Results

Increasing competition for shrinking government budgets for research and the disproportionately large rewards for publishing in the best journals have exacerbated the temptation to fudge results or ignore inconvenient data.

Massaged results can send other researchers down the wrong track, wasting time and money trying to replicate them. Worse, in medicine, it can delay the development of life-saving treatments or prolong the use of therapies that are ineffective or dangerous. Malpractice comes to light rarely, perhaps because scientific fraud is often easy to perpetrate but hard to uncover.

The field of psychology has come under particular scrutiny because many results in the scientific literature defy replication by other researchers. Critics say it is too easy to publish psychology papers which rely on sample sizes that are too small, for example, or to publish only those results that support a favoured hypothesis. Outright fraud is almost certainly just a small part of that problem, but high-profile examples have exposed a greyer area of bad or lazy scientific practice that many had preferred to brush under the carpet.

Many scientists, aided by software and statistical techniques to catch cheats, are now speaking up, calling on colleagues to put their houses in order.

Those who document misconduct in scientific research talk of a spectrum of bad practices. At the sharp end are plagiarism, fabrication and falsification of research. At the other end are questionable practices such as adding an author's name to a paper when they have not contributed to the work, sloppiness in methods or not disclosing conflicts of interest.

"Outright fraud is somewhat impossible to estimate, because if you're really good at it you wouldn't be detectable," said Simonsohn, a social psychologist. "It's like asking how much of our money is fake money—we only catch the really bad fakers, the good fakers we never catch."

If things go wrong, the responsibility to investigate and punish misconduct rests with the scientists' employers, the academic institution. But these organisations face something of a conflict of interest. "Some of the big institutions . . . were really in denial and wanted to say that it didn't happen under their roof," says Liz Wager of the Committee on Publication Ethics (COPE). "They're gradually realising that it's better to admit that it could happen and tell us what you're doing about it, rather than to say, 'It could never happen.'"

There are indications that bad practice—particularly at the less serious end of the scale—is rife. In 2009, Daniele Fanelli of the University of Edinburgh carried out a meta-analysis that pooled the results of 21 surveys of researchers who were asked whether they or their colleagues had fabricated or falsified research.

Publishing his results in the journal *PLOS ONE*, he found that an average of 1.97% of scientists admitted to having "fabricated, falsified or modified data or results at least once—a serious form of misconduct by any standard—and up to 33.7% admitted other questionable research practices. In surveys asking about the behaviour of colleagues, admission rates were 14.12% for falsification, and up to 72% for other questionable research practices."

A 2006 analysis of the images published in the *Journal of Cell Biology* found that 1% of accepted papers have at least one image that has been manipulated in a way that affects the interpretation of the data—though the authors made no conclusions about intent.

Rise in Retractions

According to a report in the journal *Nature*, published retractions in scientific journals have increased around 1,200% over the past decade, even though the number of published papers had gone up by only 44%. Around half of these retractions are suspected cases of misconduct.

Wager says these numbers make it difficult for a large research-intensive university, which might employ thousands of researchers, to maintain the line that misconduct is vanishingly rare.

New tools, such as text-matching software, have also increased the detection rates of fraud and plagiarism. Journals routinely use these to check papers as they are submitted or undergoing peer review. "Just the fact that the software is out there and there are people who can look at stuff, that has really alerted the world to the fact that plagiarism and redundant publication are probably way more common than we realised," says Wager. "That probably explains, to a big extent, this increase we've seen in retractions."

Ferric Fang, a professor at the University of Washington [Medical Center] and editor in chief of the journal *Infection and Immunity*, thinks increased scrutiny is not the only factor and that the rate of retractions is indicative of some deeper problem.

He was alerted to concerns about the work of a Japanese scientist who had published in his journal. A reviewer for another journal noticed that Naoki Mori of the University of the Ryukyus in Japan had duplicated images in some of his papers and had given them different labels, as if they represented different measurements. An investigation revealed evidence of widespread data manipulation and this led Fang to retract six of Mori's papers from his journal. Other journals followed suit.

Self-Correction

The refrain from many scientists is that the scientific method is meant to be self-correcting. Bad results, corrupt data or fraud will get found out—either when they cannot be replicated or when they are proved incorrect in subsequent studies—and public retractions are a sign of strength.

That works up to a point, says Fang. "It ended up that there were 31 papers from the [Mori] laboratory that were retracted, many of those papers had been in the literature for five–10 years," he says. "I realised that 'scientific literature is self-correcting' is a little bit simplistic. These papers had been read many times, downloaded, cited and reviewed by peers and it was just by the chance observation by a very attentive reviewer that opened this whole case of serious misconduct." . . .

Scientists who try to replicate and confirm previous studies find it difficult to get their research published. Scientific journals want to highlight novel, often surprising, findings. Negative results are unattractive to journal editors and lie in the bottom of researchers' filing cabinets, destined never to see the light of day.

"We have a culture which values novelty above all else, neophilia really, and that creates a strong publication bias," says [Chris] Chambers [a psychologist at Cardiff University]. "To get into a good journal, you have to be publishing something novel, it helps if it's counter-intuitive and it also has to be a positive finding. You put those things together and you create a dangerous problem for the field." . . .

In some cases, misconduct (or fraud) has grave implications. In 2006, Anil Potti and colleagues at Duke University reported in the *New England Journal of Medicine* that they had developed a way to track the progression of a patient's lung cancer with a device, called an expression array, that could monitor the activity of thousands of different genes. In a subsequent report in *Nature Medicine*, the same scientists wrote about a way to use their expression array to work out which drugs would work best for individual patients with lung, breast or ovarian cancer, depending on their patterns of gene activity. Within months of that publication, the biostatisticians Keith Baggerly and Kevin Coombes of the M.D. Anderson Cancer Center in Houston had their doubts, and began uncovering major flaws in the work.

"It looked so promising that they actually started to do trials of cancer patients, they chose the chemotherapy depending on this test," says Wager. "The test has turned out to be completely invalid, so people were getting the wrong therapy, because the paper was not retracted quickly enough."

Despite Baggerly and Coombes raising the alarm several times with the institutions involved, it was not until 2010 that Potti resigned from Duke University and several of the papers referring to his work on the expression array were retracted. "Usually there is no official mechanism for a whistleblower to take if they suspect fraud," says Chambers. "You often hear of cases where junior members of a department, such as PhD students, will be the ones that are closest to the coalface and will be the ones to identify suspicious cases. But what kind of support do they have? ... That's a big issue that needs to be addressed." ...

The Economics of Science

The pressure to commit misconduct is complex. Arturo Casadevall of the Albert Einstein College of Medicine in New York and editor in chief of the journal *mBio*, places a large part of the blame on the economics of science. "What is happening in recent years is that the rewards have become too high, for example, for publishing in certain journals. Just like we see the problem in sports that, if you compete and you get a reward, it translates into everything from money and endorsements and things like that. People begin to take risks because the rewards are disproportionate." ...

Casadevall and Fang are aware that their spotlight on misconduct has the potential to show up scientists in a disproportionately bad light—as yet another public institution that cannot be trusted beyond its own self-interest. But they say staying quiet about the issue is not an option.

"Science has the potential to address some of the most important problems in society and for that to happen, scientists have to be trusted by society and they have to be able to trust each other's work," Fang says. "If we are seen as just another special interest group that are doing whatever it takes to advance our careers and that the work is not necessarily reliable, it's tremendously damaging for all of society because we need to be able to rely on science."

For Simonsohn, the biggest issue with outright fraud is not that the bad scientist gets caught but the corrupting effect the work can have on the scientific literature. To reduce the potential negative effects dramatically, Simonsohn suggests requiring scientists to post their data online. "That's very minimal cost and it has many benefits beyond reduction of fraud. It allows other people to learn things from your data which you were not able to learn about, it allows calibration of other models, it allows people to, three years later, reanalyse your data with new techniques."

Ivan Oransky, editor of the Retraction Watch blog that collects examples of retracted papers, argues: "The reason the public stops trusting institutions is when [its members] say things like, 'There's nothing to see here, let us handle it,' and then they find out about something bad that happened that nobody handled. That's when mistrust builds." The big challenges that face humanity, says Casadevall, are scientific ones—climate change, a new pandemic, the fact that most of our calories are coming from a very few plants, which are susceptible to new pests. "These are the big problems and humanity's defence against them is science. We need to make the enterprise work better."

| "Those who are attacking [sociologist Mark] Regnerus cannot admit their true political motives, so their strategy has been to discredit him for conducting 'bad science.'"

Sometimes Scientists Are Accused of Misconduct for Political Reasons

Christian Smith

In the following viewpoint, Christian Smith discusses the case of sociologist Mark Regnerus, who at the time the viewpoint was written was being investigated by his university because of allegations of scientific misconduct. Smith, who had supervised the research done by Regnerus, attests that it was done properly. In Smith's opinion, there was no misconduct and the accusation was made solely for political reasons by opponents of the study's conclusions. Smith points out that many social scientists have strong opinions and do not respect the right of others to disagree with them. Regnerus has since been cleared by the university, which stated that good faith differences in interpretations of data are not misconduct. Smith is a professor of sociology and director of the Center for the Study of Religion and Society and the Center for Social Research at the University of Notre Dame.

As you read, consider the following questions:

1. On what grounds does Smith conclude that the research done by Regnerus did not involve any misconduct?

2. According to Smith, what besides fair treatment for Regnerus is at stake when scientists attack others because of political objections to the results of their research?

3. How, in Smith's opinion, should controversial research results be dealt with?

Who ever said inquisitions and witch hunts were things of the past? A big one is going on now. The sociologist Mark Regnerus, at the University of Texas at Austin, is being smeared in the media and subjected to an inquiry by his university over allegations of scientific misconduct.

Regnerus's offense? His article in the July 2012 issue of *Social Science Research* reported that adult children of parents who had same-sex romantic relationships, including same-sex couples as parents, have more emotional and social problems than do adult children of heterosexual parents with intact marriages. That's it. Regnerus published ideologically unpopular research results on the contentious matter of same-sex relationships. And now he is being made to pay.

In today's political climate, and particularly in the discipline of sociology—dominated as it is by a progressive orthodoxy—what Regnerus did is unacceptable. It makes him a heretic, a traitor—and so he must be thrown under the bus.

Regnerus's study was based on a nationally representative sample of adult Americans, including an adequate number of respondents who had parents with same-sex relationships to make valid statistical comparisons. His data were collected by a survey firm that conducts top studies, such as the American National Election Studies, which is supported by the National Science Foundation. His sample was a clear improvement over those used by most previous studies on this topic.

Regnerus was trained in one of the best graduate programs in the country and was a postdoctoral fellow under an internationally renowned scholar of family, Glen Elder, of the University of North Carolina at Chapel Hill. (Full disclosure: I was chair of Regnerus's dissertation committee.) His article underwent peer review, and the journal's editor stands behind it. Regnerus also acknowledges the limitations of his study in his article, as he has done in subsequent interviews. And another recent study relying on a nationally representative sample also suggests that children of same-sex parents differ from children from intact, heterosexual marriages.

But never mind that. None of it matters. Advocacy groups and academics who support gay marriage view Regnerus's findings as threatening. (As an aside, that is unnecessary, since his findings can be interpreted to *support* legal same-sex marriage, as a way to counter the family instability that helps produce the emotional and social problems Regnerus and others have found.)

Regnerus has been attacked by sociologists all around the country, including some from his own department. He has been vilified by journalists who obviously (based on what they write) understand little about social-science research. And the journal in which Regnerus published his article has been the target of a pressure campaign.

The Larger Context

The Regnerus case needs to be understood in a larger context. Sociologists tend to be political and cultural liberals, leftists, and progressives. That itself is not a problem, in my view. (I am not a conservative.) A critical progressive outlook is part of sociology's character and contribution to the world, making

Regnerus Vindicated by University of Texas

The University of Texas at Austin has determined that no formal investigation is warranted into the allegations of scientific misconduct lodged against associate professor Mark Regnerus regarding his July article in the journal *Social Science Research*.

As required by its Revised Handbook of Operating Procedures, the university conducted an inquiry to determine whether the accusations made by writer Scott Rose had merit and warranted a formal investigation. After consulting with a four-member advisory panel composed of senior university faculty members, the Office of the Vice President for Research concluded in a report on Aug. 24 that there is insufficient evidence to warrant an investigation. . . .

The allegations raised by Rose fall under the university's definition of scientific misconduct, which states, in part, that "ordinary errors, good faith differences in interpretations or judgments of data, scholarly or political disagreements, good faith personal or professional opinions, or private moral or ethical behavior or views are not misconduct."

As with much university research, Regnerus' New Family Structures Study touches on a controversial and highly personal issue that is currently being debated by society at large. The university expects the scholarly community will continue to evaluate and report on the findings of the Regnerus article and supports such discussion.

"University of Texas at Austin Completes Inquiry into Allegations of Scientific Misconduct," University of Texas press release, August 29, 2012.

it an interesting and often useful discipline, especially when it comes to understanding poverty and inequality, determining whether social policies are effective, and establishing why education systems succeed and fail. But the ideological and political proclivities of some sociologists can create real problems.

Many sociologists view higher education as the perfect gig, a way to be paid to engage in "consciousness raising" through teaching, research, and publishing—at the expense of taxpayers, donors, and tuition-paying parents, many of whom thoughtfully believe that what those sociologists are pushing is wrong.

It is also easy for some sociologists to lose perspective on the minority status of their own views, to take for granted much that is still worth arguing about, and to fall into a kind of groupthink. The culture in such circles can be parochial and mean. I have seen colleagues ignore, stereotype, and belittle people and perspectives they do not like, rather than respectfully provide *good arguments* against those they do not agree with and *for* their own views.

The temptation to use academe to advance a political agenda is too often indulged in sociology, especially by activist faculty in certain fields, like marriage, family, sex, and gender. The crucial line between broadening education and indoctrinating propaganda can grow very thin, sometimes nonexistent. Research programs that advance narrow agendas compatible with particular ideologies are privileged. Survey textbooks in some fields routinely frame their arguments in a way that validates any form of intimate relationship as a family, when the larger social discussion of what a family is and should be is still continuing and worth having. Reviewers for peer-reviewed journals identify "problems" with papers whose findings do not comport with their own beliefs. Job candidates and faculty up for tenure whose political and social views are not "correct" are sometimes weeded out through a subtle (or obvious), ideologically governed process of evaluation, which is publicly justified on more-legitimate grounds—"scholarly weaknesses" or "not fitting in well" with the department.

To be sure, there are many sociologists—progressives and otherwise—who are good people, scholars, and teachers. But the influence of progressive orthodoxy in sociology is evident in decisions made by graduate students, junior faculty, and even senior faculty about what, why, and how to research, publish, and teach. One cannot be too friendly to religion, for example, such as researching the positive social contributions of missionary work overseas or failing to criticize evangelicals and fundamentalists.

The result is predictable: Play it politically safe, avoid controversial questions, publish the right conclusions.

Those who are attacking Regnerus cannot admit their true political motives, so their strategy has been to discredit him for conducting "bad science." That is devious. His article is not perfect—no article ever is. But it is no scientifically worse than what is routinely published in sociology journals. Without a doubt, had Regnerus published different findings with the same methodology, nobody would have batted a methodological eye. Furthermore, none of his critics raised methodological concerns about earlier research on the same topic that had greater limitations, which are discussed in detail in the Regnerus article. Apparently, weak research that comes to the "right" conclusions is more acceptable than stronger studies that offer heretical results.

What Is at Stake

What is at stake here? First, fair treatment for Regnerus. His antagonists have already damaged his chances of being promoted to full professor. If his critics are successful at besmirching his reputation, his career may be seriously damaged.

But something bigger is at stake: The very integrity of the social-science research process is threatened by the public smearing and vigilante media attacks we have seen in this case. Sociology's progressive orthodoxy and the semicovert activism it prompts threaten the intellectual vitality of the discipline, the quality of undergraduate education, and public trust in academe. Reasonable people cannot allow social-science scholarship to be policed and selectively punished by the forces of activist ideology and politics, from any political quarter. University leaders must resist the manipulation of research review committees by nonacademic culture warriors who happen not to like certain findings.

Science already has its own ways to deal with controversial research results. Studies should be replicated. Data sets should be made public and reanalyzed. And new and better studies should be conducted. Eventually the truth comes out. By those means, Regnerus might be shown to have been wrong or perhaps be vindicated. That is how science is supposed to work.

By contrast, political attacks like those on Regnerus are contemptible and hurt everyone in the long run, including progressives. Everybody—specially officials at the University of Texas at Austin—needs to be vigilant in protecting scholars and their research against those inside and outside of academe who seek to silence scholars whose research runs counter to the current orthodoxy.

Periodical and Internet Sources Bibliography

The following articles have been selected to supplement the diverse views presented in this chapter.

Yudhijit Bhattacharjee	"The Mind of a Con Man," *New York Times Magazine*, April 26, 2013.
Michael Brooks	"Scientists Behaving Badly," *Huffington Post*, April 24, 2012.
Hashem Dbouk	"'Publish or Perish' and the Plague of Scientific Misconduct," *ASCB Post*, October 18, 2013.
Daniele Fanelli	"Why Growing Retractions Are (Mostly) a Good Sign," *PLOS Medicine*, December 3, 2013.
Charles Gross	"Disgrace: On Marc Hauser: A Case of Scientific Misconduct at Harvard," *Nation*, January 9, 2012.
James Hicks	"Opinion: Ethics Training in Science," *Scientist*, May 14, 2013.
Carolyn Y. Johnson	"Harvard Investigation of Stem Cell Scientific Misconduct Provides Insight into Secretive Process," *Boston Globe*, April 8, 2013.
Thomas H. Lüscher	"The Codex of Science: Honesty, Precision, and Truth—and Its Violations," *European Heart Journal*, April 2013.
Stephanie Pappas	"Men Commit More Scientific Fraud than Women," LiveScience, January 22, 2013.
Helen Thomson	"Stem Cell Scientists Reveal 'Unethical' Work Pressures," *New Scientist*, March 28, 2014.
Ed Yong, Heidi Ledford, and Richard Van Noorden	"Research Ethics: 3 Ways to Blow the Whistle," *Nature*, November 27, 2013.

For Further Discussion

Chapter 1

1. According to Annalee Newitz, cutting government-funded scientific research is detrimental to the future of the United States. What reasons does the author give for making this argument? Do you think Newitz's reasoning is sound? Explain.

2. David Eisenberg argues that cuts in government funding hurt scientific research and the economy. Do you agree with Eisenberg? Why, or why not?

3. Michael D. Tanner contends that medical research should not be funded by the US government. In your opinion, if the US government ceased funding medical research, would this help or harm medical advancements? Defend your answer.

Chapter 2

1. Richard A. Epstein questions whether technological innovation can endure government regulation. Based on the viewpoint, do you believe technological innovation can survive while being regulated? Why, or why not?

2. Jon Entine claims that tight regulations are hampering stem cell research. Does Entine provide sufficient evidence to support his claim? Explain your answer.

Chapter 3

1. The American Anti-Vivisection Society (AAVS) argues that using animals in research is unethical and unreliable. What are some reasons for this argument? Do you agree with the AAVS's argument? Why, or why not?

2. According to Ross R. Keller, research on animals has led to advances in medicine. Do you believe medicine would be as advanced as it is today without animal research? Defend your answer.

3. George Dvorsky believes that new technologies are emerging that may eliminate animal experimentation. What are some examples of these technologies? In your opinion, would these innovations end animal experimentation? Why, or why not?

Chapter 4

1. The Associated Press and Richard B. Primack report on scientific research fraud and misconduct. The Associated Press claims that fraud is escalating, while Primack contends that misconduct is extremely rare. With which author do you agree, and why?

2. Alok Jha asserts that fraud and misconduct are a threat to scientific research. In your opinion, what actions can be taken to curb fraud and misconduct in the research community? Explain.

3. Christian Smith maintains that researchers who publish unpopular findings are sometimes unjustly accused of misconduct for political reasons. Based on the viewpoint, do you think this trend will continue? Explain your reasoning.

Organizations to Contact

The editors have compiled the following list of organizations concerned with the issues debated in this book. The descriptions are derived from materials provided by the organizations. All have publications or information available for interested readers. The list was compiled on the date of publication of the present volume; the information provided here may change. Be aware that many organizations take several weeks or longer to respond to inquiries, so allow as much time as possible.

American Association for Laboratory Animal Science (AALAS)
9190 Crestwyn Hills Drive, Memphis, TN   38125-8538
(901) 754-8620 • fax: (901) 753-0046
e-mail: info@aalas.org
website: www.aalas.org

The American Association for Laboratory Animal Science (AALAS) is a professional membership association that believes the use of laboratory animals in scientific and medical research is essential to the improvement and protection of the quality of all life. To that end, AALAS advocates humane care and treatment of laboratory animals and advances responsible laboratory animal care. Its publications include the quarterly *Laboratory Animal Science Professional*, the *Journal of the American Association for Laboratory Animal Science (JAALAS)*, and the international journal *Comparative Medicine (CM)*.

Animal Welfare Institute (AWI)
900 Pennsylvania Avenue SE, Washington, DC   20003
(202) 337-2332 • fax: (202) 446-2131
e-mail: awi@awionline.org
website: www.awionline.org

The Animal Welfare Institute (AWI) is a nonprofit organization founded in 1951 to reduce pain inflicted on animals by humans. AWI advocates for the humane treatment of laboratory animals and the development and use of non-animal testing methods. It encourages humane science teaching and the prevention of painful experiments on animals by students. AWI publishes *AWI Quarterly* in addition to books, pamphlets, and online articles such as "Sea Change Afloat for Chimpanzees in Laboratories."

Earthwatch Institute

114 Western Avenue, Boston, MA   02134
(978) 461-0081 • fax: (978) 461-2332
e-mail: info@earthwatch.org
website: www.earthwatch.org

The Earthwatch Institute is a nonprofit organization founded in 1971 to engage citizens worldwide to participate in scientific field research. Additionally, it seeks to promote the understanding and action necessary for a sustainable environment. It supports scientific research on wildlife and ecosystems, ocean health, climate change, biodiversity, archaeology, and paleontology. Its website features the *Earthwatch Unlocked* blog, as well as articles, reports, and a downloadable version of its "Expeditions 2014" booklet.

Foundation for Biomedical Research (FBR)

1100 Vermont Avenue NW, Suite 1100
Washington, DC   20005
(202) 457-0654 • fax: (202) 457-0659
e-mail: info@fbresearch.org
website: fbresearch.org

The Foundation for Biomedical Research (FBR) is an organization that supports humane animal research. It serves to inform and educate the public about the necessity and importance of laboratory animals in biomedical research and testing. FBR publishes a semiannual magazine, *ResearchSaves*, as well as a daily e-newsletter, *Total E-Clips*. Its website offers articles such as "Pigs, Transplants and Stem Cells" and "Blood Pressure Reduced in Rats—New Hope for Patients."

Humanity+

5042 Wilshire Boulevard, Suite 14334, Los Angeles, CA   90036
e-mail: info@humanityplus.org
website: humanityplus.org

Humanity+ is an international nonprofit organization that seeks to develop knowledge about the science, technology, and social changes of the new millennium. It advocates the ethical use of technology to elevate human capabilities and heighten human enhancement. It supports discussion and public awareness of emerging technologies and defends the rights of individuals to adopt such technologies for the well-being of all humans. It publishes the quarterly *H+ Magazine*.

Medical Research Modernization Committee (MRMC)

3200 Morley Road, Shaker Heights, OH   44122
(216) 283-6702
website: www.mrmcmed.org

The Medical Research Modernization Committee (MRMC) is a national health advocacy group made up of physicians, scientists, and other health care professionals who evaluate and promote efficient, reliable, and cost-effective research methods. MRMC-sponsored activities include research, publishing, and student education. MRMC's website offers several reports, including "A Critical Look at Animal Experimentation" and "Of Pigs, Primates and Plagues: A Layperson's Guide to the Problems with Animal-to-Human Organ Transplants."

National Academy of Sciences (NAS)

500 Fifth Street NW, Washington, DC   20001
(202) 334-2000
website: www.nasonline.org

Established in 1863, the National Academy of Sciences (NAS) is a society of distinguished scholars engaged in scientific research and dedicated to the use of science and technology for the good of society. Made up of more than two thousand members, the NAS offers independent, objective advice on matters related to science and technology. Among its many publications are the weekly serial *Proceedings of the National Academy of Sciences of the United States of America (PNAS)* and the quarterly *Issues in Science and Technology*, which features articles such as "Is U.S. Science in Decline?"

National Institutes of Health (NIH)

9000 Rockville Pike, Bethesda, MD   20892
(301) 496-4000
e-mail: NIHinfo@od.nih.gov
website: www.nih.gov

The National Institutes of Health (NIH) is part of the US Department of Health and Human Services and is the primary federal agency for conducting and supporting medical research in the United States. NIH funds thousands of scientists in universities and research institutions throughout the country and the world. Many resources are available on its website, including "NIH Policies and Procedures for Promoting Scientific Integrity."

National Science and Technology Council (NSTC)

Eisenhower Executive Office Building
1650 Pennsylvania Avenue, Washington, DC   20504
(202) 456-6055
e-mail: nstc@ostp.gov
website: www.whitehouse.gov/administration/eop/ostp/nstc

The National Science and Technology Council (NSTC) is a cabinet-level council within the executive branch of the US government. The council coordinates science and technology policy across the entities that make up the federal research and development enterprise. One of the goals of NSTC is to establish clear national goals for federal science and technology investments. NSTC publishes various reports, including "Priorities for Accelerating Neuroscience Research Through Enhanced Communication, Coordination, and Collaboration."

National Science Foundation (NSF)
4201 Wilson Boulevard, Arlington, VA   22230
(703) 292-5111
e-mail: info@nsf.gov
website: www.nsf.gov

Created by Congress in 1950, the National Science Foundation (NSF) is an independent federal agency that works "to promote the progress of science; to advance the national health, prosperity, and welfare; and to secure the national defense." The agency is the funding source for approximately 24 percent of all federally supported basic research conducted by US colleges and universities. NSF offers many publications on its website, including "Survey of State Government Research and Development: FYs 2010 and 2011" and "Reducing Investigators' Administrative Workload for Federally Funded Research."

Office of Science and Technology Policy (OSTP)
Eisenhower Executive Office Building
1650 Pennsylvania Avenue, Washington, DC   20504
(202) 456-4444
website: www.whitehouse.gov/administration/eop/ostp

Established by Congress in 1976, the Office of Science and Technology Policy (OSTP) advises the president of the United States and others within the executive office on the effects of science and technology on domestic and international affairs. OSTP advises the executive office on the implementation of budgets, policies, plans, and programs related to science and technology. The OSTP Resource Library provides a variety of speeches, documents, presentations, reports, and testimony, including "Statement of Dr. John P. Holdren to the Committee on Science, Space, and Technology of the United States House of Representatives on 'The President's FY2015 Budget Request for Science Agencies.'"

Union of Concerned Scientists (UCS)
2 Brattle Square, Cambridge, MA   02138-3780
(617) 547-5552 • fax: (617) 864-9405
website: www.ucsusa.org

The Union of Concerned Scientists (UCS) was founded in 1969 by a group of scientists and students at the Massachusetts Institute of Technology to promote science in the public interest. UCS opposes US government political interference in scientific research and promotes free speech rights for federal scientists. The UCS website features *The Equation* blog and offers articles such as "Timeline of Abuses of Science" and "Heads They Win, Tails We Lose: How Corporations Corrupt Science at the Public's Expense."

Bibliography of Books

Nancy Baron — *Escape from the Ivory Tower: A Guide to Making Your Science Matter.* Washington, DC: Island Press, 2010.

Kathryn Bayne and Patricia V. Turner, eds. — *Laboratory Animal Welfare.* Waltham, MA: Academic Press, 2013.

Alex Berezow and Hank Campbell — *Science Left Behind: Feel-Good Fallacies and the Rise of the Anti-Scientific Left.* Washington, DC: Public Affairs, 2012.

Elizabeth Popp Berman — *Creating the Market University: How Academic Science Became an Economic Engine.* Princeton, NJ: Princeton University Press, 2012.

Paula Boddington — *Ethical Challenges in Genomics Research: A Guide to Understanding Ethics in Context.* New York: Springer, 2012.

Leah Ceccarelli — *On the Frontier of Science: An American Rhetoric of Exploration and Exploitation.* East Lansing: Michigan State University Press, 2013.

Robert P. Charrow — *Law in the Laboratory: A Guide to the Ethics of Federally Funded Science Research.* Chicago, IL: University of Chicago Press, 2010.

John D'Angelo — *Ethics in Science: Ethical Misconduct in Scientific Research.* Boca Raton, FL: Taylor & Francis, 2012.

Heather E. Douglas — *Science, Policy, and the Value-Free Ideal*. Pittsburgh, PA: University of Pittsburgh Press, 2009.

K. Eric Drexler — *Radical Abundance: How a Revolution in Nanotechnology Will Change Civilization*. New York: PublicAffairs, 2013.

Jeremy R. Garrett, ed. — *The Ethics of Animal Research: Exploring the Controversy*. Cambridge, MA: MIT Press, 2012.

David Goodstein — *On Fact and Fraud: Cautionary Tales from the Front Lines of Science*. Princeton, NJ: Princeton University Press, 2010.

Lori Gruen — *Ethics and Animals: An Introduction*. New York: Cambridge University Press, 2011.

Robert C. Hubrecht — *The Welfare of Animals Used in Research: Practice and Ethics*. Chichester, UK: Wiley-Blackwell, 2014.

C. Renée James — *Science Unshackled: How Obscure, Abstract, Seemingly Useless Scientific Research Turned Out to Be the Basis for Modern Life*. Baltimore, MD: Johns Hopkins University Press, 2014.

Andrew Knight — *The Costs and Benefits of Animal Experiments*. New York: Palgrave-Macmillan, 2011.

David L. Lewis — *Science for Sale: How the US Government Uses Powerful Corporations and Leading Universities to Support Government Policies, Silence Top Scientists, Jeopardize Our Health, and Protect Corporate Profits.* New York: Skyhorse Publishing, 2014.

Thomas O. McGarity and Wendy E. Wagner — *Bending Science: How Special Interests Corrupt Public Health Research.* Cambridge, MA: Harvard University Press, 2012.

Philip Mirowski — *Science-Mart: Privatizing American Science.* Cambridge, MA: Harvard University Press, 2011.

Vaughan Monamy — *Animal Experimentation: A Guide to the Issues.* New York: Cambridge University Press, 2009.

Chris Mooney and Sheril Kirshenbaum — *Unscientific America: How Scientific Illiteracy Threatens Our Future.* New York: Basic Books, 2009.

National Research Council — *Proposed Revisions to the Common Rule for the Protection of Human Subjects in the Behavioral and Social Sciences.* Washington, DC: National Academies Press, 2014.

Barbara K. Redman — *Research Misconduct Policy in Biomedicine: Beyond the Bad-Apple Approach.* Cambridge, MA: MIT Press, 2013.

David B. Resnik   *Playing Politics with Science: Balancing Scientific Independence and Government Oversight.* New York: Oxford University Press, 2009.

Zachary M. Schrag   *Ethical Imperialism: Institutional Review Boards and the Social Sciences, 1965–2009.* Baltimore, MD: Johns Hopkins University Press, 2010.

Dane Scott and Blake Francis, eds.   *Debating Science: Deliberation, Values, and the Common Good.* Amherst, NY: Prometheus Books, 2011.

Kristin Shrader-Frechette   *Ethics of Scientific Research.* Lanham, MD: Rowman & Littlefield, 2013.

Wesley J. Smith   *A Rat Is a Pig Is a Dog Is a Boy: The Human Cost of the Animal Rights Movement.* New York: Encounter Books, 2012.

Paula Stephan   *How Economics Shapes Science.* Cambridge, MA: Harvard University Press, 2012.

Ivan Valiela   *Doing Science: Design, Analysis, and Communication of Scientific Research.* New York: Oxford University Press, 2009.

Harold Varmus   *The Art and Politics of Science.* New York: Norton, 2009.

David Vogel   *The Politics of Precaution: Regulating Health, Safety, and Environmental Risks in Europe and the United States.* Princeton, NJ: Princeton University Press, 2012.

Index

Global warming. *See* Climate change research

Gluck, John, 155

Goldacre, Ben, 63

Google, 31–32

Gorillas, 118

Government influence and oversight

    areas of research, 18, 22, 25, 34, 36, 51, 197, 199

    funding, and research integrity policy, 176, 203, 204, 209

    funding cooperatively with private sources, 97

    funding cuts, and effects, 21, 22–23, 43–47, 56, 57–59, 67

    funding legislation, 18–20

    government-funded research is essential to public good, 22, 25, 26–27, 28–33

    government-funded research is investment in the future, 21–27

    government funding lowers quality of scientific research, 34–42

    government should not have influence, 20

    high-profile NSF projects, 26, 31–32, 36

    history and gains, 22, 25, 29

    institutional review boards, 62

    medical research, and politics, 48–52, 57, 97, 109

    myths addressed, 21–27, 35

    regulation of government-funded research is justified, 75–81

    See also Regulation; US Congress

Great Ape Protection and Cost Savings Act (bill), 148

Greely, Hank, 109–110

Griffith, Thomas, 95

Gruen, Lori, 139–143

Gun violence studies, 51

H

Hackam, D.G., 129

Haida peoples, 100

Hamburger, Philip, 63

Hather, Gregory J., 25

Head injury research, 63

Hepatitis, 159

HIV research, 57, 123, 125, 157, 159

H5N1 avian influenza, 112–115

Holdren, John, 111–115

Honesty and dishonesty, 179, 181–182

    See also Misconduct and fraud

Hong Kong, 90

Howard Hughes Medical Institute, 44

Hubble telescope, 22

Human experimentation

    animal research as alternative, 121, 123, 125, 150

    clinical trials, pharmaceuticals, 125, 126, 129–130, 131

    consent, 177

    ethics, 62–63, 123, 150

    regulation, 62–63, 65, 72, 156

    stem-cell research, 180, 204

Human immune systems

    Ebola studies, 118

    virtual systems, and research, 156–157